THE WATERMAN'S WIDOW

A True Story

THE
WATERMAN'S WIDOW

A True Story

by Carol McCabe Booker

New Bay Books

THE WATERMAN'S WIDOW
by Carol McCabe Booker

Editor
Sandra Olivetti Martin
New Bay Books
Fairhaven, Maryland
NewBayBooks@gmail.com

Cover Design by Suzanne Shelden

Photo collage by Suzanne Shelden: Engraved portrait of a woman from page 20, *WOMEN: A Pictorial Archive from Nineteenth-Century Sources, 488 Copyright-free Illustrations for Artists and Designers,* selected by Jim Harter, Dover Press. Combined with: Oyster tonger fishing from stern, Chesapeake Bay, Md., c1905; Library of Congress Prints and Photographs Division; https://loc.gov/pictures/resource/cph.3b13954/

Interior design by Suzanne Shelden
Shelden Studios
Prince Frederick, Maryland
sheldenstudios@comcast.net

A Note on Type: Cover and section heads are set in Walden Font Type No. 2; The text font is ITC Bookman Std.

Library of Congress
Cataloging-in-Publication Data

ISBN 979-8-9853477-8-4

Printed in the United States of America
First Edition

DEDICATION

Digging into the history of events described in this book was both fascinating and frustrating. Because the transcript of the murder trial is missing, almost all we know about the midnight shooting on Solomon's Island on September 13, 1900 is from detailed newspaper reports. None of those dispatches identified the reporters. Their coverage brought to light a tragic event in what was then a very rural watermen's community, a far cry from the popular destination of sightseers, vacationers, and seafood lovers that it is today. This book is dedicated to those and countless other journalists the world over, whose faithful reports on events large and small, good and evil, help preserve our history—and so often without even a byline.

TABLE OF CONTENTS

PROLOGUE

The sudden gunshot was heard up to a mile away. But to many of the sleeping islanders, it sounded like anything but that. The next morning some said they had just rolled over, dismissing the momentary breach of the midnight peace as either the figment of a dream or a mate's snores. Some of those who recognized it as a gunshot despite the haze of sleep questioned its meaning since it was mid-September and the bird hunting season, highly popular on the Chesapeake Bay and neighboring marshes, was still weeks away. But only the few in close proximity leaped from their beds, anxiously dressing to investigate. Because after that brief pop, they had also heard the short, shrill, female cry. Was there a madman on the island? A feud being settled? Either was so unlikely on Solomon's Island, a tranquil, waterman's community. By daybreak they would learn the source of the shot.

But would they ever know who fired it?

1

AN OMINOUS FORECAST

A man's gotta love it to do it.

—A Chesapeake Waterman

It was the last week of summer 1900, the start of the oyster season on the Chesapeake Bay. From its headwaters north of Baltimore to points some 200 miles south, almost a quarter of a million Marylanders made their living plowing those waters. For many of them, including some 600 or so souls on southern Maryland's Solomon's Island, the oyster industry was their chief means of support. Now, at the opening of the 1900–1901 season, the outlook was never more dismal. The Bay's once abundant oyster beds were disappearing, and unless steps were taken to prevent it, near-total depletion was a reasonable possibility. The total yield in the past year was under a million bushels, as compared with almost two million bushels a decade earlier in the 1890–91 season. Weighing this more than 50 percent decrease, experts at the U.S. Fish Commission (a forerunner of the Interior Department's Fish and Wildlife Service) concluded that "at this rate, in twenty years the industry will have acquired absolute insignificance."

Supporting that dim prediction, the September opening of the new season was disappointing. A local newspaper in Calvert, the southern Maryland county with a long shoreline along the Bay, summed it up in two sentences:

> *Warm weather is preventing any activity in the oyster business, which opened the season last Saturday. The demand is light and the market has not assumed any definite shape.*

On Solomon's Island, Dr. William H. Marsh, the community's first doctor, was also a volunteer weather observer. He reported from his home at the island's tip, overlooking the confluence of the Patuxent River and the Bay, that September temperatures had reached an uncomfortable high of 97 degrees on September 5. Warm temperatures can hinder growth and prompt fewer oysters to spawn. There were also thunderstorms on September 14, 16, 26 and 27, and total rainfall for the month was 3.05 inches. None of this was good for oystering. To watermen, these conditions signaled a continuing period of decline in the bounty of the Chesapeake.

The Fish Commission described the Bay as "one of the richest agricultural regions of the earth, the fertility of its bottom being comparable only to that of the valleys of the Nile and Ganges." But the Bay was adapted for one crop only: oysters. The Chesapeake alone yielded twice as many oysters as all foreign countries put together. Given time, and with substantial investment, the Commission predicted that the slow death of the industry could be turned around. Toward that end, in April 1900, the Maryland legislature enacted a law banning oystering on three creeks around Solomon's Island—Mill, St. Johns and Back Creeks—for three years, due to the depleted condition of beds formerly rich in oysters. The experts estimated that with proper cultivation, the oyster-growing areas in the Chesapeake would be worth $100 an acre yearly (the equivalent of more than $3500 in 2023 dollars). But the depletion of the oyster beds had already affected the livelihoods of local watermen around Solomon's Island and nearby waters, and many were in debt.

The Tongers

The oysterman's work was back-breaking, hands-on labor. The tools used to pull the shellfish from the floor of the Bay were the oyster tongs. Picture two sticks, up to 30 feet in length, and crossed at a pivot point like scissors about a quarter of the way from one end. The heads of the tongs resemble rakes: a set of claws and bars spaced to allow small shells and debris to fall out, but not the oysters.

The waterman kept his boat loosely anchored so that each time he lowered the tongs, the rake scraped a different spot on the bed. The scissor movement of the tongs broke the oysters loose from the bed and raked them into a pile. He then grasped the pile with the coupled rakes and brought the loaded tongs up, dumping the oysters on a culling table to be sorted by size.

This was the preferred method of oystering, although some watermen insisted instead on dredging the beds. They pulled a submerged basket behind the boat for a half mile or so, unavoidably damaging the beds while harvesting the oysters. The dredgers persisted in this method even after both Maryland and Virginia banned it, while the tongers viewed them with unbridled disdain.

Whatever the method of harvesting, the peaceful quest for oysters turned into a war. From 1865 until the mid–1900s, licensed watermen and pirates feuded up and down the Chesapeake Bay and on both the Potomac and Patuxent rivers. In 1830, Maryland banned nonresidents from harvesting oysters in its waters, then prohibited dredging, and ultimately required annual permits for oystering.

After the Civil War, the demand for oysters soared wildly, bringing fishermen from as far away as New England down the coast and up into the Bay and its tributaries. There, they clashed with Marylanders and Virginians, who were already battling each other on the beds. The *St. Mary's Beacon* reported in the spring of 1877 that "quite a number of Eastern 'Yankee' schooners" had been in the Patuxent River in the past ten days for oysters to plant in their Northern and Eastern waters, "but not one" had been allowed to carry a single bushel from the river. The article credited the "Oyster Police," a force created by Maryland in 1868, with preventing the poaching.

Violence between tongers and dredgers, as well as the depletion of the oysters, led Virginia to ban dredging in 1879. Still, pirates from both states plundered each other's coastal oyster beds, some continuing to use the illegal method. Many of the watermen carried concealed weapons.

By the 1900 season, many of the local oystermen had given up altogether. Between the 1896 and 1901 oyster seasons, the number of tongers licenses issued in Calvert County declined almost 34 percent (from 897 to 594). Some of those who persisted were turning to the upper Bay, where the oysters seemed more plentiful, while others still plugged away on the shallow bars lining the creeks and inlets around the island where harvesting was still permitted. Only those with incomes from other than—or in addition to—oystering had any money to invest in the purchase of oyster beds, as the Commission recommended.

Even in the best of times, when he enjoyed a good harvest and wasn't confronting poachers, an oysterman's life was not always smooth sailing. He went out on the water on the coldest winter days, when the wind turned his face a raw red and the water froze his fingers as he worked the tongs. It was often said that a man had to love it to do it. Yet one never heard anyone say he loved it. The oyster tonger had no reason to expect a long life, but these days, he would be a fool to expect an easy one. The oysters were disappearing, and along with them, his livelihood.

This was the context of the mysterious shooting in the minutes after midnight in a small, rundown home on Solomon's Island Road on September 13, 1900.

2

MYSTERIOUS SHOOTING AT SOLOMON'S ISLAND

SECRET MURDER AND ROBBERY

*The victim fatally shot while in his bed
beside his sleeping wife and child*

The *Baltimore Sun* reported the incident in a single sentence on the front page: "Capt. Littleton T. Condiff was mysteriously shot in the head and fatally wounded while in bed in his house in Calvert County." Further details would follow the next day in a "Special Dispatch" to the *Sun* under the headline "Died Of His Wound," over a tower of subheads referring to a "secret murder and robbery" and stating that the victim had been sleeping beside his wife and child. The newspaper reported that Capt. Condiff had been shot Wednesday night, and that he had died of the wound at 2:30 in the afternoon on Friday:

> *The bullet passed into his brain through
> the right eye, producing paralysis and
> unconsciousness. His wife was in bed
> beside him when he was shot, and their
> child was in the same room.*

The wife says she was awakened just before midnight by the report of the firearm and found that her husband was wounded. She says no one was in the room at the time except her husband, herself and the child.

The newspaper further reported that no weapon had been found in the room. The victim was said to be about 50 years of age, a "mariner" engaged in the oyster business. He was not known to have had any enemies, being "regarded as a worthy citizen of Solomon's Island." There was, however, a possible motive provided by the wife, whose name was not included in the article:

His wife stated that he had about $200 [equivalent to more than $7,000 today] in cash in the house. This money could not be found after his death. From this fact it is supposed that robbery was the motive for the murder.

It is conjectured that Captain Condiff was aroused by the robber's entrance and was shot as he raised himself up in bed while the wife and child slept, and that the assassin then made his escape before his presence could be detected. But this is only conjecture.

While its depiction of the murder itself was admittedly conjecture, the newspaper's initial description of the scene differed in several curious details from evidence gathered in the ensuing investigation, including testimony taken at the coroner's inquest. Beyond the first news report, for example, there was never any mention of a child being in the bedroom when the captain was murdered.

"Oyster Packing House of the World"

The murder victim, Littleton T. Condiff, 51, was one of the Solomon's oystermen confronting the stark realities of the upcoming season in September 1900. Like most of the population on the two-square-mile island, he made his living off the bounty of the Chesapeake Bay.

Sometime in the mid–1870s, "Lit," as he was called by family and close friends, joined the scores of watermen who followed their dreams to Solomon's Island. Like many others, he was lured from Hungary Neck, in Somerset, Maryland's southernmost county, on the Bay's Eastern Shore. Like Solomon's, Somerset was home to a community of oystermen who worked the harbors, inlets, and shoals along the Bay. Lit was seeking his fortune by heading west—in this case north by northwest. A young man in his 20s, he was eager for a new life on an island in the Patuxent River, less than 50 nautical miles away, which promised more prosperity to oystermen than any other point in the middle Bay.

Even the island's name sprang from this enterprise: the oyster cannery established in 1865 by Isaac Solomon. Solomon had bought all seventy or more acres of what was then known as Sandy Island, established a cannery, and lured watermen to live and work there, even building homes for them. Tradition has it that when oystermen started saying they were hauling their loaded bushel baskets to "Solomon's," years later shortened to simply "Solomons," the name caught on.

What Lit found on Solomon's Island in the 1870s was enough to convince him to make the western shore community his home for the rest of his life. A description written at the time by a visitor to the island might help explain why. The anonymous writer of a letter to the editor of the *Baltimore Sun* had made the overnight trip down the Bay from Baltimore on the steamer *Mary Washington* at the invitation of Capt. M.L. Weems, the well-known owner of a Patuxent line of steamboats. Steamboats had appeared on the Bay around 1813, built by a shipyard in Baltimore. By mid-century they were the primary means of transportation between that port and all major points south.

Landing at the wharf at the tip of the island, the correspondent was met by Charles Solomon, Isaac's son and resident member of the oyster packing firm that was converting the tiny sand spit into an industry hub. Charles Solomon invited the visitor to his home, about 100 yards from the wharf, for an "excellent" breakfast of soft-shell crabs and mint julep. He then toured the island, taking copious notes to share with the *Sun*'s readers. At times sounding like a real estate ad, the resultant letter described the island as "prettily located" near the mouth of the Patuxent River, where it was intended by its new owner to be "the oyster packing house of the world."

The factory the Solomons operated was capable of steaming and packing four thousand bushels of oysters daily, according to Charles Solomon. Touring the facility, the correspondent saw plates marked "Patented by Isaac Solomon" on a variety of labor-saving machinery, bearing witness to the innovative genius behind the operation. There was also a separate building where ten to fifteen men were at work making one- and two-pound cans for packing oysters, and in the off-season, fruits and vegetables. Nearby were thirty-five homes occupied by families employed in the factories, and fifteen more were scheduled to be built.

One of these homes was bought by Capt. Lit and his wife in 1884, a purchase made possible by successful oyster seasons since his arrival on the island. Nearby was Isaac Davis' boatyard, soon to be the largest on the Bay, and much more. Besides a number of churches of various denominations, built or about to be built on land donated by Isaac Solomon, there was a public school with fifty students. The school term commenced May 1 and ended November 1, thus reversing the usual order of holidays, to allow children who were old enough to work during the winter and spring shucking and packing oysters. All five Condiff children would eventually attend the school, although Harris, the eldest boy, would drop out after nine years, not uncommon for teenage boys.

There was a resident physician on the island, as well as a justice of the peace and constable. The visitor reported, however, that "the officers of the law complain of a dearth of business." That proved true throughout the remainder of the century, which made Capt. Condiff deem Solomon's Island a good place for a waterman to live and raise a family. It would also make his murder on a mid-September night in 1900 utterly incomprehensible.

The correspondent closed by noting that if the much-anticipated railroad line to nearby Drum Point were completed [it never was], "this place will be of immense value, located as it is in the finest harbor of the known world."

Whatever went wrong, Isaac Solomon's cannery was not successful. On August 4, 1875, all of his holdings, comprising almost the entire island, were offered at public auction. The oyster industry, however, continued to thrive for at least another fifteen years, when it began a potentially fatal decline.

TRUSTEE'S SALE
OF
VALUBLE REAL ESTATE AND GROUND RENTS AT
"SANDY ISLAND," NOW CALLED "SOLOMON'S ISLAND,"
CALVERT COUNTY, MARYLAND,
IMPROVED BY ABOUT TWENTY-SIX DWELLING HOUSES.

By virtue of a decree of the Circuit Court of Calvert County, sitting as a Court of Equity, the undersigned, as Trustee, will offer for sale at public auction, on the premises, on WEDNESDAY, the 4th day of August, 1875, at 4 o'clock, P. M.,

ALL THAT TRACT, PART, OR PARCEL OF LAND, situated in Calvert County, Maryland, formerly called "Sandy Island," now called "Solomon's Island," near the mouth of the Patuxent River, containing SEVENTY ACRES OF LAND, more or less, being part of the same land which by deed dated 27th November, 1865, and recorded among the land records of Calvert County in Liber D. B. M. D., No. 2, folio 32, &c., was granted and conveyed by Susannah L. Fitzgerald, Committee and Trustee, unto Isaac Solomon, saving and excepting, however, one quarter of an acre, which by deed dated the 22d August, 1870, and recorded among the land records of Calvert County in Liber S. S., No.2, folio 53, was conveyed by Isaac Solomon to Jacob Breden et al. for Church purposes.

The said seventy Acres, more or less, are improved by ten DWELLING HOUSES, cottage style, eleven two-story Frame DWELLING HOUSES, three one-and-a-half-story Frame DWELLING HOUSES, one two-story cottage style DWELLING HOUSE, one one-and-a-half-story large STOREHOUSE AND FACTORY BUILDINGS.

ALSO,
ALL THE FOLLOWING GROUND RENTS issuing out of Ten Acres of Land, more or less, on the said Island, viz:

ONE IRREDEEMABLE GROUND RENT OF SEVENTY DOLLARS, payable half-yearly on the first days of March and September, arising out of one acre, three roods and thirty-one perches of land, more or less, by virtue of a lease from Isaac Solomon unto Solomon & Son and Davis, dated 10th March, 1870, and duly recorded. Improved by a MARINE RAILWAY, STOREHOUSE and several small DWELLING HOUSES, and all the following REDEEMABLE GROUND RENTS.

Difficult Times

Only after the coroner's inquest into Capt. Littleton Condiff's death did Baltimore newspaper reports on the murder include the name of the victim's wife. It was "Bessie," born Elizabeth Miller Tarlton. At first described simply as a "strong woman," Bessie was about eight years his junior. They had married in 1876, the original record lost in the fire that destroyed the courthouse in Prince Fredericktown in 1882. Bessie had grown up in Baltimore, the daughter of Solomon Mitchell Tarlton and Isabelle Richardson Spalding.

The house that Lit and Bessie purchased in 1884 was a modest two-story home on Solomon's Island Road. The house occupied a perfect location, fronting west on the Patuxent River, with a rear porch overlooking Back Creek, where the waterman kept his boat tethered to a small pier. Best of all, the couple owned it free and clear. That made Lit proud and gave Bessie a sense of security. But that was only until 1895, when the declining oyster harvests, plunging every year since 1890, had so submerged the couple in debt that they were forced to mortgage their home.

Reporters who covered the murder described the Condiff home as one of the smallest, most rundown houses on the island. Its poor condition was no doubt the result of the financial hardships the family had endured over the past decade.

When they'd bought the house, they already had three of their eventually five children—Mary, Isabelle

Virginia (nicknamed Virgie), and Harrison (or Harris, as the family called him). (Bessie had also lost two pregnancies.) By the time of Capt. Condiff's death in 1900, they had two more children, Albert, 11, and Philip, 8. The two girls had both married watermen and were living on their own, Mary (Mrs. Clarence Greenfield) in Baltimore, and Isabelle (Mrs. Andrew Johnson) on Solomon's. Harris, now 17, was also working on the water; his two younger brothers were in school.

By this time, the mortgage was five years in arrears. The annual payment of $102 plus interest had never been made. The final payment was due in a few months, on February 4, 1901. The mortgage was held by J. F. Webster, himself a waterman originally from Somerset County, but a successful entrepreneur as well. The family also had a large tab at Webster's store, the go-to general store on Back Creek that not only had just about everything islanders needed but also was known for carrying many of their customers in hard times, the Condiffs among them. At this point, many of the island's watermen were in the same dire financial straits.

Lit expected Harris, as the couple's first son, to follow him as an oysterman. Right now, his job was to help the captain with culling the shellfish, tending to the baskets, and otherwise acting as mate on the family's small boat. It was obvious, however, that Harris hated it. He wanted nothing to do with the hard life of a tonger. But at his young age, and with the family facing such hard times, he had little choice.

Harris had heard enough about Baltimore from his maternal grandmother to believe it would be a better place to live, with many more opportunities than he'd ever have on tiny, rustic Solomon's. And much more excitement, Bessie's mother, Isabel (better known as Mary) Tarlton, who had been living with the family on Solomon's for several months, had filled his head with vivid images of the big city, the largest port on the Chesapeake. He'd learned from her that his grandfather, Solomon Tarlton, at one time had been a mover and shaker in city politics during the presidential campaign of 1860. That is, until he inexplicably stole a valuable horse from a stable out in Howard County. According to the evidence presented at trial, Tarlton, a Baltimore resident, had ventured out into the countryside some 11 miles and in the dark of night entered the stable and took the horse, together with a saddle and bridle. He had ridden to Lancaster, Pennsylvania, more than 70 miles away, where he was pursued and arrested, the horse still in his possession.

Tarlton was convicted and sentenced to jail in 1862. His defense had relied heavily on character references, specifically, the subpoenaed testimony of a number of politicians who, he maintained, could attest to his sterling character and reputation. The bottom fell out, however, when none of the subpoenaed pols appeared. They had told the sheriff sent to fetch them that they knew nothing of Tarlton except having met him at several city conventions and other party events. The trial also revealed that he had a prior record and had served time in the penitentiary before 1850.

After serving his term for the horse theft, Tarlton again did the unthinkable, and was sent back to the penitentiary on eight counts of burglary. Although he died before Harris and his other grandchildren were born, his widow's stories about his exploits, apparently recasting him in the boy's eyes as a daring thrill seeker, stirred visions of a life more exciting than anything Solomon's Island could ever offer.

There were times when even feeding their three growing boys may have been more than the Condiffs could handle. However, other family members were available to help out, from time to time taking in the younger boys in exchange for their help with babysitting or household chores. That may have explained the boys' absence on the night of the murder.

Life Insurance

One bill the couple never failed to pay was the periodic assessment for Capt. Condiff's life insurance. He was determined that whatever happened to him—and the possibilities were unpredictable in the extremes of wintry weather on the Chesapeake—his family would be financially secure. In 1895, he joined the Heptasophs, a popular fraternity that issued life insurance policies to its members. Capt. Condiff took out an insurance policy in the amount of $2,000 [equivalent to over $70,000 today]. He even served for a year or more as the chapter's treasurer.

The Improved Order of Heptasophs (from the Greek "Seven Wise Men") was one of the first five fraternities in the United States to popularize the fraternal insurance business. The society had split from the original Order of Heptasophs, founded in Louisiana in 1852. The breakup reportedly arose over the question of whether the order should offer life insurance. The dissidents believed it was an important part of fraternal life and broke away to form their own society. Chartered in Baltimore in 1878, the Improved Order was one of the largest of the nation's fraternities, and its stability was said to compare favorably with any of the others by the turn of the century.

The "Heps," as they were familiarly called, stressed the importance of a man protecting his dear ones at a time when it was most sorely needed, citing the biblical passage that decries a man who does not provide for his own as worse than an infidel. Ages of admission were between 21 and 55. To maintain its own solvency, the fraternity required a medical exam showing the applicant to be in good health. It also prohibited the establishment of new branches in areas where there were serious health problems, including most of the southern states, due to sporadic epidemics of yellow fever.

Members paid periodic assessments during the year toward life insurance benefits ranging from $1,000 to $5,000, payable at death. A $2,000 policy such as Capt. Condiff's would cost about $15 annually, payable in eleven assessments of $1.36 over twelve months. (That annual premium is the equivalent of just over $500 today, a hefty burden on a waterman in a time of scarce productivity and low income.) The captain and Bessie had never failed to make a payment.

The Heptasoph justification for such sacrifice was eloquently defined in a eulogy by the Supreme Prelate at an annual service for departed members in the early 1900s:

> *The mere fact that a man is a Heptasoph is a great point in his favor. It demonstrates convincingly that he lives for others than himself. A selfish person makes a poor Heptasoph. He realizes that he has a duty to perform after his soul has burst its mortal cerements and fled to elysian fields. He is a better father, brother and husband because he is a Heptasoph, for in its conclaves he is taught that he owes a duty to those who are dependent upon him that cannot be lightly regarded. A Heptasoph recognizes that there will come a time when his strong arms and virile physical strength will fail, and,*

apprehending that dread time, he makes provision that those whose lives are linked with his shall not become a burden upon the bounty of society. This, to us, represents the highest type of civilization.

The News Spreads

Throughout the island and beyond, news of the shooting spread rapidly. Capt. Condiff was still breathing on Thursday evening when watermen, returning from a disappointing day working the tongs on low-yielding oyster beds, heard the awful details about the gunshot that had pierced the night. It was the only topic of conversation among the mariners who gathered at Webster's store after tying up for the night. All day long, women had slipped into each other's homes up and down the island to share whatever news they'd heard and speculate as to its meaning. The Solomon's Chapter of the Daughters of America, a secret, nativist society, passed the news among its members. (Founded in the 1880s, the fraternal organization's mission ranged from preserving the public school system to protesting against the immigration of "paupers, criminals, and the enemies of our social order.") The quiet and reserved Bessie had been a trustee of the chapter.

Even the *Baltimore Sun*, more than 70 miles north, had received a "special dispatch." The paper described the mysterious shooting as "the number one conversation among residents."

The local *Calvert Journal,* a weekly published in Prince Frederick, the county seat, reported that "the peaceful town of Solomon's was thrown into wild excitement" by the announcement that Capt. Littleton Condiff, "one of its best known residents," had been shot while sleeping in his bed. Solomon's, it noted, was a prosperous little town with "an enviable reputation for good order and morality." Any kind of disturbance, the paper observed, was most unusual, and "this affair has therefore caused more than ordinary excitement and comment."

Lit had a brother on the island, George, two years his junior, who lived nearby with his wife, Kate, and their three children. George and his elder son, just 18, were both watermen. But by 1900, feeling the impact of the declining oyster harvest, they were looking for other means of making a living. Eventually that quest would include turning their home on the Patuxent into a popular and prosperous guest house (the Locust Inn) that hosted distinguished visitors from Washington, DC, and beyond.

Right now, like many others on the island, the family was in shock. They waited in stunned confusion and concern as Lit lingered in his bed, teetering between life and death. At 2:30 p.m. on Friday, September 14, his family at his bedside, Capt. Condiff, without ever having regained consciousness, finally succumbed to the bullet hole in his brain. Then, like everyone else, his brother and sister-in-law wanted answers.

3

CORONER'S INQUEST

*At first light this dawn, the Old Captain has
died; let him live on in legend tonight!*
—Old Sea Chanty

*In the history of Solomon's Island,
no record of such a crime as this.*

In keeping with Maryland law and practice, a coroner's inquest into the mysterious death of Capt. Littleton Condiff was convened the very next day. Until 1939, when the state established a Department of Postmortem Examiners, it was this official who investigated suspicious or violent deaths. The coroner's office was generally considered of importance equal to that of the sheriff. In fact, in the event of certain disabilities of the sheriff, the coroner could act for him, although it rarely happened.

The Maryland Code provided that with certain exceptions, a coroner was to summon a jury of inquest over the body of any deceased person who came to his death by accident, mischance, or as the result of an apparent felony. Whenever it appeared that a person had died as a result of violence, the justice could also require the attendance of a physician to examine the victim to determine the cause of death and to testify and give evidence of his findings.

Under Maryland common law, the coroner was required to convene the inquest at the very place where the death had occurred. Furthermore, if anyone were found guilty by the jury of inquest, the coroner was to commit him (or her) to jail to await trial.

On Solomon's Island, this power was vested in William H. Files, who grew up on the island, became active in Democratic Party politics, and was also a justice of the peace, appointed by a succession of governors. His full-time occupation, however, was "confectioner," operating the ice cream parlor next door to the public school on Patuxent Avenue, the ribbon running along the southern tip of the island.

Patuxent Avenue from River, Showing Public School, Solomons, Md.

Files' first act in this case was to issue a search warrant on September 15, authorizing Calvert County Sheriff Harrison C. Long to search the dwelling of the deceased waterman. The warrant was based on the sworn statement of State's Attorney J. Frank Parran that he had probable cause to suspect that money, deadly weapons, or other things concealed in the dwelling might lead to the discovery of the person or persons who committed the murder. The sheriff returned the warrant the same day, reporting that there was "Nothing found." He had actually conducted the search the day before, without waiting for the warrant.

Just 32, J. Frank Parran was an up-and-coming figure in Maryland politics. A graduate of Charlotte Hall Military Academy, he had studied law at the University of Virginia before returning to Calvert County and becoming active in the Republican Party. He was only 29 when he was appointed superintendent of Calvert County Schools, a position he held just three years before nailing the post he really wanted—States Attorney for Calvert County—which he held for the next twenty years. The Condiff murder was the first big case of his career. He would spare no effort to crack it.

Parran's first step was to assign a local attorney, William H. Hellen, to take charge of the investigation immediately after the shooting, pending his own arrival in Solomon's from Prince Frederick. Hellen, a Democrat, was a prominent lawyer who had served two terms in the Maryland legislature. Described in the press as a "fluent talker" and a "man active in church circles," he had also run twice unsuccessfully for both the U.S. Congress and the Maryland Senate as a Prohibitionist in the 1880s. He was currently serving as counsel to the Oystermen's Mutual Protective Association of Calvert, lobbying for laws to protect the industry and the watermen of Calvert County.

Parran also dispatched a detective, Isaac Spandauer of the well-known Baltimore detective agency, Smith, West & Lyons, to Solomon's to work the case. The involvement of the famous private investigators was enough to intensify interest in any case. Founded in 1862, by the end of the century the firm was known from coast to coast for its successes in bringing back bank robbers, forgers, embezzlers, and other headline-grabbing criminals to face justice in Baltimore courts. Spandauer was one of their top detectives.

The excitement on Solomon's was palpable. From the oyster boats to the quilting bees, there was no other topic of discussion. Every eye on the island focused on the proceedings called to order by Coroner Files on Saturday morning. There had been mysterious deaths discovered in years past, but they were usually drownings, and typically found to be accidental. There had never been anything like this on Solomon's Island.

The First Witness: Dr. Marsh

Coroner Files swore the jury and then summoned Dr. Marsh as the first witness. Slim and straight-backed, the bespectacled physician approached the witness chair with his usual air of authority. There was not a sound in the room as the respected surgeon began his testimony. He told the jury he had been summoned to the Condiffs' home about 1 a.m. by 17-year-old Harris Condiff, who told him that his father had been shot. Upon his arrival at the house, just a short distance up the road from his own at the southern tip of the island, Dr. Marsh said he found Mrs. Condiff moaning by the side of her husband, who was lying motionless on the left side of the bed, nearest the open window, a bullet wound clearly visible in his head. He testified that she told him she had been awakened by a noise in the room, but saw no one. He also testified that Mrs. Condiff told him there was no gun in the house.

There was little the doctor could do for the waterman, who succumbed to his wound slightly more than twenty-four hours later. At that point, Dr. Marsh stated, he had performed an autopsy, which revealed a ".32-caliber pistol ball" in Capt. Condiff's brain. According to the report in the *Baltimore Sun* the next day:

> *He then testified that the nature of the wound clearly showed the following facts: First, that the pistol had been held within six inches of the man's head when it was fired; second, that he was shot while sleeping, his eyes being closed; third, that he was shot in the side of the head next to his wife.*

Dr. Marsh, according to the news report, "was positive that the pistol was held directly over the right eye of the man and that the person who fired it did so from the right side of the bed," where Mrs. Condiff claimed to be sleeping.

The newspaper reported that State's Attorney Parran seized upon this testimony as conclusive evidence that the shot could not have been fired from the window or from the side of the bed upon which Capt. Condiff was sleeping. According to the reporter, Mr. Parran "proved" that in order to shoot Capt. Condiff in the way described by Dr. Marsh, an outsider would have had to go on Mrs. Condiff's side of the bed, lean over her, and hold the pistol perpendicularly. That, he argued, was entirely improbable if the shooter's purpose was either robbery or murder, and then to get out of the house without being seen by Mrs. Condiff.

Sheriff Long testified that he had made a thorough search of the house and premises on Thursday as Capt. Condiff lay dying and had found a gun in an upstairs bureau drawer. However, it was a .22 caliber pistol, not a .32.

The Widow Testifies

The jurors sat grim faced and riveted to their seats as Bessie Condiff was called to testify. Although the newspaper had earlier reported remarks she had allegedly made about the crime scene, the *Sun* now reported that this was the first time since the death of her husband that she "could be induced to talk," and appeared to do so without reserve. After being sworn to tell the truth, she testified for nearly an hour, answering "with perfect composure the numerous questions fired at her." Her "coolness and courage," according to the reporter, were remarkable, "astonishing the authorities in charge of the case." "She tells a straight story, sticks to it, and gives no sign of weakening, in spite of the fact that evidence of the most damaging sort" was being brought out against her:

> *Mrs. Condiff said her husband had given her some time ago the sum of $200 to keep*

for him, and that he had that amount in the house when he was killed. She went on to say that on Wednesday night, after some discussion, Capt. Condiff was determined to buy oysters for planting and had asked her for some of the money, apparently half. She gave it to him and claimed that he placed the money under the mattress on his side of the bed, after which they retired for the night.

The jurors stared, eyes fixed on the widow as she calmly continued:

I had just fallen asleep, it seemed, when I was aroused by a loud noise. I rose up in bed and saw at once something the matter with Lit. I thought he had had another attack of vertigo and screamed for help. My son, Harris, and my mother, who slept upstairs, came down. My mother lit the lamp, and we all saw what had happened.

Bessie paused for a moment, as if visualizing the scene she described, while determined to maintain her composure before continuing:

When I was aroused by the shot I saw no one either in the room or leaving it, nor did I hear any other sound. When I went to look for Lit's money under the

*mattress, it had disappeared. The other
$100 I have sewed in my skirt.*

State's Attorney Parran pounced on Bessie's suggestion that someone had extracted $100 from beneath the mattress on which Capt. Condiff's 200-pound frame reposed. Attorney Hellen also questioned the plausibility of her story when he asked her whether she thought it possible for a man to lean over her, shoot Capt. Condiff, and get away without her seeing him. Bessie's blue eyes suddenly came to life with emotion. She shot back at the lawyer, "Do you think I am a fool?"

Responding to further questioning, she denied having quarreled with her husband, and said he had no enemies.

The Neighbors Take the Stand

Other witnesses provided little or no support for Bessie's scenario, except to confirm that the couple was not known to quarrel and appeared happily married. A neighbor, also a waterman, Capt. J.W. Lusby, testified that he heard the shot, and that Mrs. Condiff did not scream until five minutes later. His wife said she heard the scream and ran across the yard to her neighbor, "whom she found already dressed and not greatly agitated." Mrs. Lusby testified that she stayed with Mrs. Condiff until Dr. Marsh arrived.

Identified by the reporter as "a more important witness," another neighbor, Mrs. Jane Webster, described as living in the next house on the north side, followed Mrs. Lusby on the stand. Mrs. Webster told the jury that on Wednesday afternoon (just hours before the murder), Mrs. Condiff came to her house and said she wanted to talk to her:

> *She had never been in my house before, and I thought it very unusual. But I went downstairs and she at once asked me if my husband was a member of the Independent [sic] Order of Heptasophs.*

The jurors' attention was locked on the witness's every word as Mrs. Webster continued:

> *I told her no, and she said her husband was insured in that order for $2,000 and she was greatly worried, as she had heard a number of members had dropped out. She talked for some time about other things, and just before she left said she had a heavy burden on her mind and did not know what she would do.*

Jane Webster's testimony was the first suggestion of another possible motive for this murder, and the jury did not miss it. Bessie Condiff later denied ever mentioning it to Mrs. Webster, but acknowledged the existence of the insurance policy.

The Waterman's Son

Taking the stand next was the Condiffs' son, Harris, who corroborated much of his mother's testimony about having money in the house. He said his mother had told him, in case anything happened to her, that she had $200. He also denied all knowledge of a pistol in the house. This statement was shortly called into question, when a shop owner, Perry Evans Jr.—also a "Hep" and a past Archon (Director) of the Order—told the jury that he had sold Harris Condiff a used .32 caliber pistol "in good condition" for 50 cents (the equivalent of almost $18 today) the previous Christmas.

Recalled to the stand, Harris admitted buying the pistol, but said it was no good and he had never fired it. In fact, he said, he had taken it apart and thrown the pieces away. Upon cross-examination, he admitted he might have put the pieces on a shelf in the kitchen. In any case, he claimed no knowledge of what became of the gun or its parts.

A gun like this would have sold new for about $2.99 in 1900, so the pistol Harris purchased for 50 cents would have been a bargain if it were in good condition. Its uses, however, were limited. A pistol designed for that size bullet lacked both the accuracy and power for hunting. Even at close range, if fired at a rabbit, for example, it was more likely to wound than to kill it humanely. It was certainly useless for one of the islanders' seasonal passions: wildfowl hunting. These guns were small and built for concealment, making them a popular choice on both sides of the law.

Perhaps because many watermen during the oyster wars of the 19th century had started carrying guns for self-defense against oyster bed pirates, Harrison's reason for purchasing the pistol may not have been pursued. There was no such testimony reported by the newspapers.

The Talk on the Island

Mrs. Lusby was called back to the stand and pressed as to what else she recalled. She then testified that Mrs. Kate Condiff, wife of the deceased's brother George, had told her, "I don't care who did it, man or woman, I will be one of the first to help lynch them." There was not a sound in the room. The coroner called a recess for the night. The jurors would reconvene in the morning after Capt. Condiff's burial at 9 a.m. The Heptasophs were handling that.

Throughout the evening and the following morning, the murder was virtually the only topic of conversation on the island. Everyone, it seemed, had his or her own theory of what had happened. As for Bessie's suggested robbery motive, some neighbors found it incredible that Capt. Condiff would have had $200 at this time of year. That would represent a catch of 1,000 bushels of oysters in the last season, when everyone knew he hadn't had any luck at all. Furthermore, he owed several hundred dollars and had a mortgage on his home that was seriously in arrears.

Adding to these suspicions, Thomas Moore, another oysterman, reported having been robbed two months earlier of $100, taken from his Solomon's home on a Sunday night. Shortly before this, Perry Evans, a nearby neighbor of the Condiffs, claimed to have been robbed of a like sum. (Solomon's residents tended to leave their doors unlocked as they went about daily routines.) In both cases, the thief was never found. Moore said that his $100 was in seven, new, $10 notes, and the rest in $5 bills, "one of which was particularly greasy."

When Bessie Condiff revealed the $100 she'd sewed up in her underskirt, it reportedly matched exactly the denominations described by Moore, including one "greasy note."

The Theories Coalesce

State's Attorney Parran theorized that Mrs. Condiff had stolen both Moore's and Evans' money. He speculated that she was afraid to spend it on the island, where the family's poverty was well-known. Neither, he figured, was she willing to show it to her spouse. In the end, the attorney argued, Capt. Condiff either found out and accused her, or she killed her husband so she could say she got the money from him.

Detective Spandauer's conclusions, while differing only slightly from the attorney's, also stemmed from Bessie's testimony about the money. He suggested that her husband had given Bessie the cash to hold, and after spending part of it, she was unable to give it to him when he asked for it. She killed him, Spandauer theorized, to protect herself from him.

Whichever theory any juror may have favored didn't matter. The only question the coroner's jury had to answer was whether there was probable cause to find Bessie Condiff guilty of murdering her husband and thus justify the legal proceedings that would follow. That is what they did the next morning, just hours after Capt. Littleton Condiff was laid to rest. The verdict was swift and unanimous. It was GUILTY.

4

A DARK PORTRAIT

Peculiar disposition

Ravenous reader of dime novels

The portrait several witnesses painted of Mrs. Condiff served as the canvas upon which a variety of theories were spun out, both among the islanders and in the press. While no one described the delicately framed, 42-year-old woman as a fool, they did offer unfavorable, and sometimes loaded, descriptives, calling her, for example, a person "of a peculiar disposition," who had "few friends." The *New York Sun* reported that she had long been known "as a decidedly queer woman." The newspapers also wrote that she was "subject to epileptic fits."

That term alone had negative connotations dating back to antiquity, when seizures were shrouded in fears of demonic possession. Church-going Solomon's Islanders would be familiar with the most famous reference to epilepsy in the Bible, in which Mark, Matthew and Luke each described how Jesus healed a boy with epilepsy by driving out an evil spirit. Those suffering from such events were often feared and avoided. Some of the comments made to the newspapers suggested, if not stating outright, that Bessie Condiff was somehow harboring an evil spirit. It wasn't until the first half of the 20th century that science challenged religion and superstition by identifying the real causes of seizures, ranging from high fever or low blood sugar to disruptions in the normal connections between nerve cells in the brain.

Sheriff Long provided the finishing touch. After a thorough search of the house, the lawman revealed that he had found an "immense pile of paper-back books containing detective stories of the dime-novel variety." Mrs. Condiff, the *Baltimore Sun* went on to report, was "well known all over the island as a great reader of these novels." *The Washington Post* couldn't resist the observation that the people of the island community were "at sea as to a motive," but followed that immediately with: "She had long been known to be a ravenous reader of dime novels." This, in the crime reporting parlance of the day, was not only relevant, but meant she very likely was guilty.

"Dime Novels"

For more than two decades, the "perniciousness" of the dime novel and its influence on the youth of the country were decried in the press, usually in connection with a juvenile crime. Just a year earlier, three 14-year-old boys were charged with robbing the postmaster's house in York, Pennsylvania. One was the postmaster's own son. The *Baltimore Sun* reported that the robbery was "ascribed to the reading of dime novels."

The citizens of Solomon's Island were not unaware of the insidious connection. Another *Baltimore Sun* article reported that a couple of boys had stolen a boat in Crisfield, on the Bay's Eastern Shore, and sailed across to Solomon's before being caught and spending the night in the Prince Frederick jail. The last line read, "It was stated that they were influenced to take the cruise by reading dime novels."

One review of news articles relating to boys and dime-novel "perversions" around this time turned up as many as five police cases of the kind in one day in Brooklyn, New York. Hundreds of other articles claiming similar connections were found in every part of the country, as well as in Great Britain and Germany. (Municipal authorities in Berlin, Germany, banned the sale of dime novels after an assault on a man was blamed on the accused's reading of this "perverse" fiction.)

Earlier in the decade, under the headline "DIME NOVELS DID THE DAMAGE," the *Sun* reported that three boys awaiting sentencing for a robbery had revealed that they knew the novel *Jesse James* by heart, and considered the man who shot the outlaw a "mean scoundrel." This was contrary to the intent of the scores of so-called "blood and thunder" novelists who had penned the formulaic Wild West paperbacks since the mid–1800s. While the villains were bad, a hero always emerged in the last chapter to end their outlaw capers.

Over decades, however, it became a common criticism that young boys were influenced more by the adventurous, dare-devil outlaws, than by the good guys—the heroes who put them down. More and more news reports from coast to coast bore out that criticism. As one commentator put it, it was the villainy, not the triumph of virtue, that lingered in memory. It would take "more than a good ending," in his opinion, "to vindicate the dime novel."

The few defenders of the 10-cent fictions argued that it was action and adventure, not immorality, that were the novelist's stock in trade. One critic bet that it would surprise many persons who denounced such fiction as wholly bad to know that the publisher would not permit a line or situation that might so much as suggest indecency or vulgarity. Others, however, weren't buying any defense of the genre. Fredericksburg, Virginia's *Freelance-Star*, stuck to its guns; dime novels were "wild, weird, and sometimes wicked literature." Another claimed that the "trashy, pernicious literary slop served up under the name of 'Dime Novels' and 'Ten Cent novels' " had wholly disgusted the "better class of readers."

No distinction was made between the adventurous Wild West novels that attracted young boys like magnets, and the romances and detective stories that appealed to women. Critics found the plots of the latter just as problematic, especially when the central character was an assertive woman, as was often the case. The heroine might be a scorned lover, a brokenhearted wife, a captive, or a mistress. She might have been an excellent equestrian, or even an expert with firearms. The plots dealt with everything from unhappy marriages to crimes.

This sub-genre of women's fiction grew wildly during and after the Civil War, reportedly becoming the first "bestsellers" in the country. But despite the victory of virtue over vice inevitable in the final chapter, many male critics had harsh reviews for this "cheap fiction" that women seemed to be devouring.

By 1900, the term "dime novel," whether a detective story, a romance, murder mystery, or "wild west" adventure, had simply become synonymous with trash, sensationalism and nearly all that was degrading in literature. Far worse, the term had been so frequently linked with crime in newspaper reports across the country, that describing a person as an "avid reader" of the cheap paperbacks was tantamount to declaring him or her guilty as charged. In Bessie Condiff's case, her "avid"—even "ravenous"—reading of that "trash" was now an indelible part of her public portrait.

And Worse Yet

Reporting on the jury's verdict the following day, the *Baltimore Sun* made another observation that was more than slightly prejudicial:

> *The case bears a striking similarity to that of Mrs. Reckard, who was convicted at Towson last year of killing her husband*

*while he slept. The wound in this case,
also, was on the side of the head nearest
where the wife lay.*

The "dime novel" comments were bad enough, but there could hardly have been a more potentially damaging comparison than this reference to Clementine Reckard. Most of Maryland was very familiar with the notorious, auburn-haired beauty. (More on that later.)

Convicted

Then came another verdict, but not from the coroner's jury. Theirs had already been reported. Now the newspaper claimed to report the public's verdict: "The whole island believes the woman is guilty and the feeling runs high." That conclusion may have been debatable. The next was not: "In the history of Solomon's Island, from the days of the oldest settlers, there is no record of such a crime as this."

The local *Calvert Journal* reported that there was compassion among the islanders, but not for Bessie: "Great sympathy is felt for the aged mother [Mary Tarlton] and the family of two married daughters and three young sons."

The papers also reported that sometime the same morning, a gun was suddenly found, not by the sheriff, but by two oystermen, the Condiffs' son-in-law, Clarence Greenfield, and John Railey, who discovered it in the yard outside the Condiff home, and brought it to the sheriff's attention.

As required by law, Bessie Condiff, upon the jury's verdict, was immediately arrested and taken into custody by Sheriff Long. In the ordinary course of events in such cases, the prisoner might have remained in jail in Prince Frederick, about 20 miles north, to await arraignment. But this was no ordinary case, and the Prince Frederick jail had an unfortunate history. The decision had already been made that Detective Spandauer and Sheriff Long would remove her from the county jail the next morning and take her to Baltimore. The local newspapers reported blandly that this was for her "safety," or to avoid the expense to local government of protecting her at the jail. The *Baltimore Sun* put it more bluntly: she was being taken to the Baltimore City Jail on the petition of the State's Attorney because it was "feared she would be lynched," and the Prince Frederick jail was not considered strong enough to resist such an attack. "Threats of lynching," the paper reported, had been "numerous among the inhabitants of Solomon's Island."

5

A HISTORY
OF LYNCHINGS

Our National Crime

Man or woman, it don't matter!

Talk of lynching punctuated the gossip among islanders before the coroner's inquest had even ended. It wasn't just the comment reported by Mrs. Lusby. Several neighbors had also heard Capt. Condiff's sister-in-law volunteer to lead a lynch mob. Others were making similar comments. More often than not, the speaker indicated the gender of the murderer would make no difference. "Man or woman, it don't matter!"

The State's Attorney's concerns about the Prince Frederick jail's ability to withstand a lynch mob were founded on historical fact. Fourteen years earlier, the same shoddy, two-cell building had been overrun in minutes by a mob set upon lynching Charles Whitley, described in newspapers as an 18-year-old mulatto who'd been in the jail only a few days. In their reporting and editorials, the newspapers described his alleged crime as heinous (the alleged assault of a young child), but no word of his denial or defense was ever reported. The mob had appointed itself judge, jury and executioner. The newspapers had no problem with that, some bluntly condoning the lynching. The *Calvert Gazette*, for example, contended:

> *While we have able and impartial judges to preside over our courts, justice is so often defeated by the confusing methods employed by crafty counsel in defense of criminals, and our laws allow of so many technicalities behind which a criminal may seek refuge, that an unfortunate distrust of justice in such cases has arisen in the public mind, and to which may be attributed the frequent resort to lynch law. While we deplore the tragedy that has occurred in our county, yet the offense that led to it must strike us all as deserving a terrible punishment.*

Another lynching only four years before the Condiff murder must also have weighed into Parran's decision to remove Bessie to Baltimore, even though it happened about 38 miles west of Prince Frederick in neighboring Charles County. There were significant similarities between the two cases, including the race of the accused murderers—both White, a rarity in the history of Maryland lynchings. Equally noteworthy, the case involved the murder of a spouse in bed in the middle of the night, and the accused husband's defense, like Bessie's, was that an intruder had committed the crime.

A Notorious Affair

Several years after the Charles County lynching of a white man, the story was still so well known that it often took no more than a passing reference to call to mind the infamous details. The obituary of Nicholas Jones, a Black tenant farmer, illustrates the point. When Jones died of pneumonia on April 21, 1899, at his home near Hilltop, in Charles County, Maryland, his passing was reported in the *Maryland Independent*, a semi-weekly published in Port Tobacco (the county seat until 1895, when it was moved to La Plata). The paper's contents reflected the area's majority African-American population, which had voted overwhelmingly for the party of Abraham Lincoln. The obituary described "Uncle Nick," as the old man was known, as "an aged and respectable colored man," adding one other significant fact about his life, which had begun in slavery 68 years earlier. But it was neither that fact, nor that he'd been one of 362 slaves drafted into the Union Army in 1864, less than a year before the end of the Civil War. Nor did the obituary mention his later life as a tenant farmer when the paper reported his routing of an unidentified dog that had been killing farmers' sheep, including eight of Jones' ewes in one day.

The one detail about Uncle Nick's life that was mentioned in the obituary was that he "was the first one to find and give information about Joe Cocking being coiled with rope in the basement of his store at Hill Top, the morning after the memorable double tragedy at that place." Nothing more needed be said about that incident because "memorable" was an understatement. The double murder in the rural hamlet just 7 miles west of Port Tobacco would never be forgotten.

The Discovery

Uncle Nick was up and out at dawn, as usual, on April 24, 1896, the start of a beautiful, spring day in Charles County. He had work to do, but he couldn't begin until he'd replaced a broken point on his plow. That was the purpose of his visit to Joseph Cocking's general store at Hilltop just as the sun was rising over the rural community. Surprised to find the front door ajar, he entered and looked around for Cocking. When he couldn't find the storekeeper, he called his name. The voice that responded seemed distant, perhaps outside, so Jones tried to follow it. After calling again, he concluded the response had to be coming from inside the store. After more callings, he traced the muffled responses to a trapdoor leading to a cellar under the store.

Opening the wooden hatch, he saw a narrow set of steps, at the bottom of which lay Joseph Cocking, bruised and bloodied, his feet bound with a length of rope. The farmer hastened down the steps, and was about to cut the rope when he noticed it was very loosely tied, and undid it instead. Cocking told him he had cut a similar bond from around his wrists by rubbing it against the edge of a broken bottle, evidence of which was later found.

Uncle Nick helped Cocking up the cellar stairs, and steadied him as he walked across the storeroom into the parlor, where he lay down on a sofa. The storekeeper then asked him to check upstairs, where his wife's and her sister's bedrooms were, saying there was "something wrong" up there. After first objecting to what seemed an inappropriate intrusion, the Black man reluctantly climbed the stairs to the second floor. Returning a minute or two later, shaken and horrified, he told Mr. Cocking that the scene upstairs was "too terrible to talk about." Cocking asked no more.

Both Mrs. Cocking, 30 years old, and her sister, 18-year-old Daisy Miller, had been murdered in their beds, gruesomely hacked about their heads with a hatchet later found on the store counter, smeared with blood.

Within hours, Joseph Cocking's story about two men—he couldn't determine their race—breaking in, attacking him and throwing him into the cellar, robbing the cash drawer, and apparently committing the murders, already was ringing hollow. Cash and jewelry both in the store and the living quarters had been left untouched. His own wounds were minor. By nightfall, the neighbors' theories about what had happened were vocal enough to make the subhead of the next day's front page story in the *Baltimore Sun*:

Some of the Neighbors Suspect the Husband and Talk of Lynching Him

The sheriff took no chances, swearing in extra deputies for duty at the Cocking home. At the same time, the storekeeper's accusers were at a loss to suggest a motive. The state's attorney asked that the best detectives be assigned to the case. Cocking, an Englishman who'd come to this country with his father as a 10-year-old, was a prosperous and popular political leader in the district. While he was said to be very jealous, relations among the Cocking family, which included three children, were at first described as "supposedly pleasant." It later appeared that the husband and wife were estranged and slept in separate rooms.

The coroner's jury met on Friday, just hours after the murder was discovered, and reconvened on Sunday, after a key piece of evidence had been found: a pair of bloody trousers hidden under the pillow of the bed Cocking had been using since the murder. These were not the pants he'd been wearing when Uncle Nick discovered him in the cellar. The jury concluded that Mrs. Cocking's murderer was her husband.

Taking him into custody, the sheriff immediately augmented the guard already protecting the man from potential mob violence, even adding a number of newspaper reporters. He put Cocking in a carriage and headed for La Plata, the county seat, followed by the deputies. Left behind at the store was a crowd of about 300 people, Black and White, many commending the jury's verdict, and some murmuring threats, hinting at, if not outrightly calling for, Cocking's lynching. Meanwhile, the funeral held for his wife and sister-in-law was the largest ever in the history of Charles County.

Perhaps realizing that the 10 miles between Hilltop and LaPlata, coupled with the vulnerability of the county jail, made him easy prey if a lynching party did form, the storekeeper asked the sheriff to take him instead to Baltimore. The sheriff put the request to the state's attorney, and after a sleepless night in the LaPlata jail, Cocking was moved to Baltimore the next day to await the grand jury.

Almost a month later, on Friday, May 22, Joseph Cocking was returned to a temporary courtroom filled with spectators in La Plata's Town Hall for arraignment on two counts of murder. He pleaded not guilty. The State indicated it would be ready for trial the following Monday. The defendant's attorney, just recently retained, requested a one-week postponement to prepare. When that postponement was denied, he asked to have the case removed on grounds that he could not get a fair trial in Charles County. The defendant later said he didn't agree with that, but it was the only way to get a delay so his lawyers could prepare his defense. The court granted the motion to remove— but not to Baltimore. Instead, the trial was moved to Leonardtown in neighboring St. Mary's County, where the court would not meet until the third Monday in September, four months away.

Public reaction was immediate and negative. The *Baltimore Sun* reported it was openly suggested that "it would be best for all sides to take Cocking to the nearest tree." At that point Sheriff Wade made the critical decision not to return Joseph Cocking to the Baltimore City Jail, despite the prisoner's friends and counsel pleading that he do so. The sheriff countered that he felt perfectly competent to protect him in Port Tobacco.

One month later, at one in the morning on Saturday, June 27, a mob took Joseph Cocking from the unguarded Port Tobacco jail and hung him from a nearby bridge.

Some later blamed the sudden mob action on alleged comments by the state's attorney that there was insufficient evidence for a conviction, a statement he vehemently denied ever making. Others saw the delay in bringing Cocking to trial as a major provocation. (In March 1900, the state legislature rushed through a law empowering circuit court judges to call the grand jury together at any time in order that cases might be brought to trial as speedily as possible.) Others claimed there'd been rumors that Cocking was planning to defame the reputation of his murdered wife, casting her as a less than pure woman. The sheriff was also blamed for asking the court to leave the prisoner in his charge instead of returning him to Baltimore.

Cocking's lynching was the fourth of a White man in Maryland. The last three occurred between 1886 and 1896, when the state saw the greatest number of lynchings in its history.

All of this influenced the decision of State's Attorney Parran and Sheriff Long to move Bessie Condiff to Baltimore as quickly as possible. But that, of necessity, would involve one night of detention in the Calvert County jail before beginning the arduous, 60-plus mile road trip to the preferred facility. For the waterman's widow, it must have seemed like the first circle of hell.

6

UNDER ARREST

A day in prison is longer than
a thousand years at large.
—Vietnamese proverb

Sheriff Long locked Bessie in one of the Calvert County jail's two cells in mid-afternoon on Sunday, September 16, just hours after her husband's body had been carried to burial by his revered Heptasoph fraternity brothers. The buggy ride from Solomon's had been more than uncomfortable due to the heavy rains a few days earlier. Trenches and gullies marred what passed for roads.

Weakened by the events of the past four days, Bessie was lifted down from the wagon, and collapsed in the heat of the cell. She lay motionless on the burlap and straw mattress spread across wooden slats atop a small, iron bed frame pressed against the wall. The journey itself had been made worse by the repetitive badgering of Detective Spandauer, riding horseback alongside the buggy.

"You might as well plead guilty," he kept saying, "everyone knows you did it." She neither looked at nor answered him, her eyes fixed either on the road ahead or closed tight in an effort to shut out the whole terrible experience. Except for sipping from a cup of tea, she had no interest in the evening meal brought to the jail by a man from Turner's Hotel.

It is possible, even likely, that Bessie Condiff spent that night entirely alone, depending on whether Sheriff Long was concerned enough to post a guard. If she slept at all, it would have been from sheer exhaustion, with the whisperings of "lynch her" seeping in and out of her consciousness. *No*, she assured herself, *they won't let that happen. Not this soon, anyway.* She anticipated descending through several more rings of hell on earth before her fate was finally decided.

Not only was the jail rarely used. The two-cell eyesore, set apart in the middle of a field behind the courthouse, was as vulnerable to attack from without as to escape from within. One commentator speculated that a prisoner would have no difficulty getting out of the Prince Frederick jail "with one well-aimed stroke of the head." Nevertheless, he continued, some never bothered to escape because other than the poor condition of his quarters, the Calvert County prisoner did not fare badly. His meals—albeit only two a day—were provided by Turner's, the only hotel in the small town of fewer than 100 residents.

The jail's location in the center of a great field allowed fresh air to enter, but only through one barred window in each cell, which provided all the air and light for the interior. The door to each cell was solid wood, admitting neither light nor air and secured by heavy locks. The two steps at the entrance to the jail allowed visitors to sit and talk to a prisoner through a cell window. Sometimes they used those windows to pass contraband, ranging from booze to weapons and tools for escape, through the same bars. The jail's vulnerability to escape also made it an easy target for any mob seeking to extract a prisoner, as had been proven just thirteen years earlier with the lynching of young Charles Whitley.

Calvert County's Nightmare

The Calvert County jail, despite several iterations over the 19th and early 20th centuries, was typically rated the worst county jail in the state. In 1843, a newspaper report described a prisoner losing his toes to frostbite after being kept in a cell without heat (a wood stove) while awaiting trial.

On March 3, 1882, a fire swept through the Calvert County seat, devouring almost every public building in slightly more than an hour—everything, that is, except the county jail. Ironically, that was the one building some people would have willingly sacrificed to the monstrous blaze. A quarter of a century later, the *Baltimore Sun* described the jail, still standing, as possibly the "least deserving of consideration from the flames." According to a newspaper report, "The only person in the jail at the time of the fire was a colored man, put there on account of an infirmity of mind. He worked well at the fire, and then contentedly went back again to his old quarters after it was all over."

In 1885, a Calvert County grand jury reported that they had examined the jail and found it "in a very bad condition—unclean, unwhitewashed, and a perfect cesspool for generating disease; indeed, unfit for a dumb animal to be put in for twenty-four hours."

The jail's poor condition not only prevailed almost two decades later, when Bessie Condiff was placed in one of its two cells for one horrifying night, but also on into the 1900s. Funding for a new jail in 1908 was so paltry that a prisoners' advocate who saw the plans predicted that the new structure would be "a disgrace to the aristocratic old county of Calvert." Among the deficiencies noted were the absence of running water in the cells, and the lack of any "bathroom in the institution." In 1926, the state director of welfare downgraded the jail's rating from "A" the previous year (when it was empty and therefore "clean and orderly") to "C" for its "very dirty and disorderly appearance." He explained, "The man in charge maintains that he is not a sheriff, and, therefore, has little authority over prisoners, as his duties comprise feeding them and the care of the building." Such an arrangement was not uncommon among the state's county jails. In Charles County, for example, an inspector found the La Plata jail was run by a 77-year-old retired courthouse janitor.

In 1936, a grand jury report described the Calvert County jail as "in a deplorably unsanitary condition," but said it was "useless" to recommend improvement as county officials insisted there were no funds available to remedy conditions. The sheriff of Calvert County didn't even have an office in Prince Frederick until 1941. A 1945 inspection reported that a widow who kept a boarding house in Prince Frederick ran the jail, "depending upon her colored handyman to do the work." But the inspector found the Howard County jail by far the worst that year, from every perspective. This was the jail where a trustee, who had the run of the jail and the warden's residence in the latter's absence, attempted to rape a 14-year-old female detainee.

As late as 1955, the Calvert County jail, although found to be "fairly clean," continued to be run by a boarding house keeper, Mrs. Mae King, who was paid 75 cents per day to feed prisoners. The Maryland State

Department of Corrections jail inspector that year issued a report finding that the situation at this jail, which he termed "a lockup only" and not secure in any way, was the worst in the state. "Men and women are locked up here and no one is in attendance most of the time. Mrs. King cannot handle the prisoners and the cleaning and feeding is generally left to her servants." Calvert was one of nine counties in which prisoners were fed only two meals a day.

Such reports prompted the publisher of the *Calvert Journal* (who was also a Trial Magistrate) to comment that the Calvert County jail was "so terrible that self-respecting criminals stay out of these parts." Calling publicity about the jail's condition "the best possible deterrent to crime in Calvert County," he urged teachers and preachers to spread the word, advising that "threats of the Calvert County jail coupled with hellfire would induce most of the wayward to mend their ways."

On Monday morning, September 17, 1900, Sheriff Long and Detective Spandauer arrived at the jail shortly after sunrise, but not before the man from Turner's had left a breakfast tray for its only inmate. Her stomach in a knot after a terrifying night filled with visions of what lay ahead, Bessie hadn't touched the food. Weak and obviously nervous, she was led by the lawmen out of the jail and helped into a buggy for the arduous trip north to Baltimore.

THE BALTIMORE CITY JAIL

There are no beautiful prisons,
nor ugly loved ones.

—French Proverb

For decades before the arrival of automobiles, Calvert County's roads were described as "bad and in many places almost impassable." Little had changed since 1882 when the horse driven to Prince Frederick by a *Baltimore Sun* correspondent (reporting on the fire), "though a powerful animal," became entangled in heavy clay in the center of the road in Prince George's County. The steed stumbled and fell, breaking the buggy.

In the drive through Anne Arundel County, gates across the road were plenty, and even where the road was winding, the traveler could see as he passed through one gate, another just ahead of him that would soon require him to again alight and go through the gate-opening process. Anne Arundel County clung to this tradition, while Calvert had adopted legislation banning road gates. Still, one occasionally found such a barrier blocking the road.

For Sheriff Long, there was no practical means other than horse and buggy to transport his prisoner to the Baltimore City Jail from Prince Frederick on Monday, September 17, 1900. The steamship line that ran the 50-mile route north to Baltimore twice a week had no scheduled stops at Dare's Wharf that day. The trip to the pier from the jail would have taken about forty-five minutes behind a good horse, and the steamer run to Baltimore about five and a half hours. This was how most county residents visited the big city. A projected rail line through the county to Drum Point, its southernmost tip, had never materialized.

The sheriff listened to State's Attorney Parran's warnings that the murmurs of lynching among Solomon's residents should not be ignored. They agreed that Bessie Condiff would be out of the County as soon as possible.

It was about 10:30 p.m. on Monday evening when the sheriff brought the buggy and its snorting steed to a halt at the entrance to the Baltimore fortress. The air temperature was in the mid-70s but the humidity, at more than 80 percent, sucked beads of sweat from every pore. The grueling trip, including necessary rest stops for both humans and horse, had taken more than twelve hours, some of it over rutted paths torn up and flooded just two days earlier by the worst wind and rain storm ever reported in Calvert County. Up and down the rolling hills lined by fields planted with crops ready for harvest or populated by grazing cows, the stallion had forged on as if deputized to do the job.

Bessie had little to say along the way, despite Detective Spandauer's taunting, urging her to confess. Witnesses at the jail described her as being "in a very nervous state," not having eaten anything for several days. She had no words for reporters who pleaded for a statement. Commenting further on her appearance, the *Baltimore Sun* observed that she was apparently used to hard work. The report continued:

> *It is now supposed that Mrs. Condiff knew her husband had some money and asked him for some. He refused, and she, becoming angry at his refusal, shot him early the next morning while he slept. Captain Condiff's life was insured for $2,000.*

So began what would stretch into more than five months incarceration in the Baltimore City Jail, before Bessie Condiff, already tried and convicted in the court of public opinion, would stand trial before a jury of her peers for the murder of her husband of twenty-four years, the father of her children.

A Dark History

The Baltimore City Jail was rebuilt in the mid-19th century by reform-minded Marylanders to correct problems such as mixing children with career criminals. The two wings of the new jail had 300 cells, gushed over by a *Baltimore Sun* editorial as "a prison in point of appearance, stability and comfort, second to none other in the country." Many of the inmates in those first years, however, were not really criminals, but runaway slaves and White Marylanders charged with helping them. While there were private jails around the harbor to house runaways, slaveholders could also pay the city jail a fee to hold them.

The cells had changed little between 1859 and Bessie's arrival in September of 1900. Their administration, however, had grown more enlightened.

The Man in Charge

While it was still a prison, in the years leading up to Bessie's incarceration, Baltimore's city jail was not as bad as many others, thanks to the man who, until recently, had stood at the helm since 1896. Warden John R. Bailey received a salary of $2,000 a year and lived rent free in a comfortable residence that appeared part of the adjacent fortress. He said that he tried to study the people in his charge, and treat them accordingly. The jail had a transient population, with a daily average of about 532, in which "peace and drunkenness" cases predominated. Many of them were repeat offenders, coming back again and again.

Warden Bailey had made a number of changes, after finding little need for corporal punishment of any sort. One innovation was adoption of a new mode of punishment, described by the jail's overseers as "of a humane character which is productive of good results." A prisoner was compelled to stand erect on a barrel for an hour for the violation of any rule of the institution, with the time lengthened for any repeat offense. Second offenses, however, were said to be rare. Another innovation was the introduction of "afternoon lectures by good volunteer talent on such subjects as will be beneficial to the adult prisoners." The warden said he'd been encouraged to do this by philanthropic people on the outside, and he believed great good could be accomplished.

Overall, according to the warden, the prisoners seldom complained about conditions, "but when they do, if there is any justice in their complaint as to the food or other things, I investigate it and do my best to remedy it." One of his remedies was the introduction of a healthier diet. The warden had also recommended a separate ward for underage prisoners. Moreover, the jail's physician reported that the facility's sanitary condition was excellent, with the addition of a hospital filling a great need.

One of the most surprising results of the warden's innovations was one prisoner's request to stay after his sentence would expire. The man had been assigned for the past two months to classifying books in the library. With his sentence almost up, he asked to remain in his present position until friends who were interested in his future welfare succeeded in procuring him some employment by which he could make an honest living. Warden Bailey recommended that his request be granted.

The warden reported, however, that "another class of prisoners who take things very hard are the better class of women who have come here through family quarrels." By late 1898, there were more women in the jail than ever before—125, of whom 22 were white and 103 "colored." A small number—perhaps four at times—would be there awaiting trial. The women did all of the jail's washing and making of clothes for the prisoners.

In 1899, Warden Bailey was forced to resign by the jail's oversight board. The majority of the board charged that he was unable to maintain discipline at the jail. Defenders of the warden retorted that members of the board visited daily, gave orders without first consulting him, and in some cases countermanded the warden's orders. Rather than resisting, Bailey announced in January that he'd decided to resign, and wished to just "fade away," having already been offered a job as manager of a trade newspaper. His successor, appointed immediately in February, did not last the year. On November 8, William R. Hall (best known for his choir singing) was dismissed for releasing prisoners either to register or to vote before being returned to the jail.

Another warden took command sometime in 1900. It made no difference to Bessie. She took every day as it came, doing whatever was expected, registering no complaints. She looked forward to visits from family members, some of whom lived in Baltimore and were caring for her two youngest children, Albert and Phillip. Christmas, 1900 was the first she had ever spent away from them, and it was exceedingly painful, as was the tenth birthday of Phillip, her youngest, on February 4. These children were too young to understand the tragedy that had befallen their family, but not to feel the pain it caused them, as well as their mother.

February also brought more and longer visits with her attorneys, selected with the advice and support of members of the family. They were probably two of the best lawyers in Calvert County, perhaps even the state.

The Lawyers for the Defense

John B. Gray, 47, had just completed a four-year term as Maryland State's Attorney for Calvert County. Born in Battle Creek, he was educated in Calvert's public schools and graduated from the Maryland Agricultural College, now the University of Maryland. He taught in Calvert schools for several years, before studying law in the office of Joseph A. Wilson, one of the most prominent lawyers in southern Maryland, state's attorney for Calvert County for four successive terms, and a state senator. Gray was admitted to the bar in 1882, and was active in Democratic Party politics.

Soon after being retained to defend Bessie, Gray brought on a young attorney named Tazewell Taylor Thomas as co-counsel. Although almost twenty years Gray's junior, Thomas, as one local newspaper put it, had already "made quite a reputation" and had a "brilliant future as a lawyer." Thomas was the son of Capt. George Thomas, a man described in his 1903 obituary as "one of the best-known residents of St. Mary's County," a veteran of the Confederate Army who'd been seriously injured at Gettysburg. Capt. Thomas had studied law but had never practiced, retiring to farming after the war. His son was making news back home as early as his junior year at St. John's College in Annapolis. His hometown newspaper reported that he'd scored "the highest average" on his exams: "4.73 out of a possible 5."

A Second Defendant

The attorneys were already on board and preparing their defense on October 20 when Gray's successor as state's attorney, J. Frank Parran, ordered Sheriff Long to make another arrest in the case. This time, it was Harris Condiff. Bessie's 17-year-old son was arrested on Sunday in Solomon's and taken to the Prince Frederick jail, the same two-cell eyesore where his mother had spent the night of September 16. The charge: accessory before the fact in the murder of Littleton T. Condiff. The basis for the charge was obviously Harris's purchase of the murder weapon the previous Christmas. He would have been held in the jail until arraignment at the Circuit Court's November term but for attorney Gray's intervention. He secured bond for the teenager, who was allowed to return home to Solomon's.

Harris's arrest may have been State's Attorney Parran's ploy to get a confession from Bessie by charging her son as an accomplice, or to get Harris to provide damning evidence against his mother. In any case, it didn't work. There wasn't enough evidence against the teen to expect the grand jury to find a presumption of guilt, despite his awkward, but not clearly perjurious, testimony at the coroner's inquest. He had indeed purchased the gun, but it was nine months before the murder, and his sworn testimony that he had tossed the cheap, previously owned pistol aside somewhere as worthless was unrefuted. The charge apparently was dropped.

For Bessie these must have been the darkest days of her incarceration, knowing that her eldest son's blunder could land him in prison for the rest of his life.

Defense counsel's next step was to prepare Bessie for the court's November term, the grand jury, and her likely arraignment. Their major concern was that the court proceedings would prompt more references in the press to the notorious Reckard case, and perhaps even further harmful comparisons of Bessie Condiff to the infamous Baltimore murderess. A brief look at Azariah Reckard's murder and his widow's trial reveals there were abundant grounds for that concern.

8

HIS DARLING CLEMENTINE: THE RECKARD MURDER

She rocked her body to and fro

An Insanity Defense

Azariah Reckard was shot and killed in the bed he shared with his wife, Clementine, in their West Baltimore home in the early morning hours of Friday, January 20, 1899. He was 38 years old. The following Tuesday morning, friends and family gathered in his brother's home on North Amity Street for a funeral service. They filled the little parlor where the black walnut coffin was covered with their floral tributes. The services were conducted by the same clergyman who had married the couple not many months earlier. Reckard's sudden death, he advised the mourners, should be a warning to others to be at all times prepared for eternity.

The one person whose absence from the gathering was most poignant was Reckard's widow. Clementine Reckard, also 38, was in the city jail. Rocking to and fro, she was crying inconsolably because she was not allowed to see her husband's body before it was buried. She'd been under suicide watch day and night, under the eyes of female attendants, with a male nearby should assistance be needed. She was refusing food, saying she had no appetite. The newspaper reported that the jail's physician and Warden Bailey, who was known for his considerate treatment of upper-class female prisoners awaiting trial, were keeping her strength up with "raw eggs and small quantities of whiskey." But it would take more than cellblock eggnog to get Mrs. Reckard through the ordeal at hand. She was charged with her husband's murder.

A Perilous Comparison

One year later, Bessie Condiff's defense attorneys, like most of Maryland, were well aware of the Reckard case, which had captured lurid headlines across the state for months. Much to the lawyers' dismay, the *Baltimore Sun* report on the Condiff murder inquest had concluded with the observation that the case bore "a striking similarity to that of Mrs. Reckard," charged the year before with killing her husband while he slept. Defense counsel's first challenge was to distance their client's public image as much as possible from Clementine Reckard's.

Mr. Reckard was killed with two bullets shot into his head—one into his brain and the other his jaw—from a seven-shot .22 caliber Smith & Wesson revolver. The small pistol was found later in the backyard. A witness would testify to selling the gun to Mrs. Reckard at his store less than twenty-four hours earlier, a purchase she denied. She claimed that the murderer was an intruder, whom she had seen and pursued. She had actually climbed out of a window in her night clothes, shouting "Fire!" and "Murder!" as she ran down the street, until picked up by the police and returned to the house. The officers found no evidence to support her bizarre account of a large man in a black slouch hat having entered the house, shooting her husband, and escaping through an open, second story window.

The widow's trial began three months later, on April 19, 1899. She'd been held in Baltimore for all but the last two weeks, which she spent in the Towson County jail. When she appeared in court, Mrs. Reckard was dressed entirely in black. A heavy crepe veil covering her face was thrown back when the proceedings began. It was, as reported by the *Baltimore Sun*, a strange scene:

> As she entered the room, she was sobbing violently and clung to her sister for support. Her face was reddened and swollen from weeping and she rocked her body to and fro, never speaking and never looking up. Her seat was moved from the chairs for witnesses to a position just behind her attorney....There she sat, her loud moans and hysterical sobbing mingling with the voices of the

lawyers. Her suffering and passionate grief half awed the throng about the rail, and they watched her in silence as she swayed and rocked without ceasing for four hours. Her daughter [by a previous marriage], sitting in another part of the room, also caught the swaying motion of the prisoner and wept unceasingly.

Jury selection consumed the entire morning, revolving around three questions:

Have you any conscientious scruples against the infliction of capital punishment?

Would it make any difference to you in your verdict whether the accused was a man or a woman?

Would you convict on circumstantial evidence if the guilt of the accused were proven beyond all reasonable doubt?

The defense also focused on whether a prospective juror was married or not. Unmarried men were quickly challenged, while panel members with grown and married daughters were readily accepted.

The Trial

After the jury was seated, the defense requested that the panel be taken to the Reckard house on Amity

Street, arguing that it was important for them to see the scene of the crime. The prosecution protested that it would be a waste of time, but the judge granted the request, saying that in a case of such gravity, he could not deny the defense's request.

After returning to the courtroom, the prosecution presented its case, introducing testimony alleging that Mrs. Reckard believed her husband was having an affair and had threatened to kill him. The defense relied on a plea of insanity, disregarding entirely the story initially told by Mrs. Reckard to the police that an unknown man had entered the house and shot her sleeping husband in his bed. Defense witnesses, including her daughter, sister, and father, in turn painted a vivid portrait of an insane woman, lacking the ability to realize the enormity of the crime with which she was charged. During the prosecution's rebuttal, that conclusion was refuted by two physicians, her late husband's brothers, the nephew who lived with the couple, and Mrs. Reckard's first husband.

After four days, the jury retired to deliberate at about nine o'clock on Saturday night. On Tuesday morning, the foreman sent word to the judge that they could not agree on a verdict. The jurors stood eight for murder in the first degree and four in the second degree, the difference being based on the question of premeditation. Not one juror had changed his vote since the first ballot on Saturday.

The Retrial

An agreement between counsel for an immediate retrial in the court's May term—a bench trial with the same judge presiding—fell apart as the proceedings were about to begin, when Mrs. Reckard changed her mind. She now refused to be tried by the judge, and declared she wanted new counsel as well. Throughout it all, she swayed and rocked, until taken from the courtroom and returned to the Towson jail.

Mrs. Reckard's second trial, begun on June 21, 1899, seemed a replay of the first, from her strange rocking to and fro, "with the regularity of a pendulum," as one newspaper put it, to the list of witnesses. Her defense counsel remained the same. One difference was that this time it took even longer to select a jury—most of the day, from 10 a.m. to 2:15 p.m. The State used all four of its peremptory challenges. The defense used all of its twenty. Both also challenged panel members for specific causes. Due to the extensive publicity around the case, most of the prospective jurors said they had already formed an opinion that could not be shaken. A number of others opposed capital punishment in the case of a woman, and some opposed capital punishment in any case.

Once the jury was seated, they were taken to the crime scene before being sequestered for the night. The State was once again seeking a verdict of first-degree murder. The defense claimed that

Clementine Reckard was insane, and for that reason would not take the stand. But they also retained her original defense—that an unknown intruder had shot her husband. This, argued the defense, was based upon truth.

The newspapers continued their detailed coverage of the trial, including one article, "Mrs. Reckard Smiles," describing how the beautiful, auburn-haired woman was apparently amused by a witness's description of her "dark red hair." Her thick, black veil was fully covering her face when the witness who claimed to have sold her the gun the day before the shooting was asked to identify her in the courtroom. At the judge's direction, Mrs. Reckard's sister lifted the folds of the veil, giving those in the room their first good look at Clementine Reckard. To their surprise, the defendant was smiling. Most of the time, even when not sobbing, she continued to sway and rock to and fro. The *Sun* reporter observed, "How the woman can continue this perpetual motion is a matter of surprise."

A common theme among the state's other witnesses was the defendant's frequent bickering with her deceased husband, in addition to alleged comments after the murder admitting guilt.

The trial lasted a full week. The jury delivered its verdict on Sunday. It was manslaughter. She would not face the gallows. The highest penalty for manslaughter was ten years in the Maryland Penitentiary.

Before announcing his sentence, the judge asked the trembling woman if she had anything to say. With a tremor in her voice, she asked that she not be sent to the penitentiary, but be allowed to serve her sentence in the Towson County Jail, where the sheriff had treated her kindly over the past four months. The judge was not moved. He sentenced her to ten years in the penitentiary.

Clementine had likely heard some of the lurid stories about Maryland's state penal institution, opened in 1811 as a maximum-security prison, and only the second of its kind in the country. In the years before that, she would have been granted her wish: Criminals were kept in the county jails or workhouses.

The penitentiary was designed to hold both males and females. Many of the buildings were scheduled for replacement in the late 1890s, but for now, the dormitory cells were described as dungeon-like, both because of their size (less than 4 feet wide by 9 feet long and 7 feet high), and the lack of windows. Some had 4-inch slits to admit light and air. The cells had no toilets or wash bowls, only "filth buckets." Building plans included larger cells (9 by 5 feet 6 inches, and 8 feet high), with a bunk, and a combination lavatory and flush toilet, which would make Maryland the first penitentiary to get rid of the filth buckets.

Clementine also was undoubtedly aware of the warden's reputation for inflicting cruel punishments on convicts—male or female—who failed to meet his standards. Those included quotas expected from the inmates as they performed their assigned tasks in the prison's contract shoe factory. That was how the prison made its money: by contracting with a shoe company to turn out its products using convict labor. The results made the warden a hit among the state's bureaucracy. As reported in the 1900 Maryland Manual: "This Institution is supported entirely by the proceeds of the labor of the prisoners, and a handsome balance is annually turned over to the State Treasury."

While a prisoner who exceeded quota could make some money for himself, if he "malingered" and failed to make his quota, he might be "cuffed up," a punishment (more accurately a torture) in which he was hauled up toward the ceiling by his handcuffed wrists, while his feet dangled above the floor. The punishment, the warden acknowledged defensively when criticized for it, was more often used on Black, rather than White, prisoners. "There are colored men—the class that generally comes here," he argued, "who cannot be made to understand anything unless it is beaten into them."

For women, punishment for misbehavior might include lockup in one of four "dark" cells, measuring just 4 by 8 feet, lacking a bed or any other furniture, and no windows or natural light. These and other abuses at the penitentiary were not revealed to the public until an investigation, prompted by a whistle-blower, after the warden's retirement. But prisoners awaiting trial for serious offenses anywhere in Maryland in the late 1800s and into the early 1900s would have heard through the grapevine what awaited them at the Maryland Penitentiary if convicted.

Since the Reckard case was so notorious, the warden greeted Clementine publicly upon her arrival at the institution's gated portal. He assured her she would be treated well if she obeyed the rules. And since she was "a rather delicate woman," he had decided to give her "light work," pasting linings in shoes. He also took the opportunity to announce that he was giving "all the prisoners a rest" that day. It was a chance for Warden Weyler to look reasonable and compassionate in the public eye, and he made the most of it.

[Clementine Reckard did behave herself, and she was released from the Maryland Penitentiary after serving about eight years of her ten-year sentence. She had been a fairly good prisoner, although she never admitted guilt in the murder of her second husband. She later married again and lived in Baltimore.]

Given this local history, Bessie Condiff's attorneys were determined to keep their client out of the newspapers as much as possible. The *Baltimore Sun* had likened the Condiff murder to the Reckard case in one of its first reports and might do it again, generating very unfavorable pretrial views of their defendant. Several newspapers also had repeatedly ended updates with speculative theories about what had happened, always concluding that Bessie had killed her husband, and even suggesting a motive, usually the insurance policy. With all of these challenges before them, making sure the woman they represented had nothing in common with Clementine Reckard was one more.

THE GRAND JURY

*A grand jury only hears one side
—the prosecutor's.*

*A grand jury would 'indict a ham sandwich,'
if that's what the prosecutor wanted.*

— A Judicial Observer

On the morning of November 13, 1900, the temperature was about 30 degrees cooler than in September when Sheriff Harrison Long had escorted his prisoner from Prince Frederick to the Baltimore City Jail. Now, as he returned her for arraignment in the Calvert County Court, road conditions were also slightly better than they had been after the almost 4-inch rainfall in forty-eight hours in mid-September. At the end of the day-long journey, Bessie was once again locked in the rundown, two-cell county jail for the night, while nearby, the grand jury met to hear the case against her.

The accused does not attend grand jury proceedings nor have the right to cross-examine witnesses. The panel does not decide guilt or innocence but whether there is enough evidence to charge someone with a crime. And unlike a trial, which is public, the grand jury proceedings are not. Exactly what each witness said will never be known, since Maryland law imposes secrecy on all grand jury proceedings. However, the word around the courthouse was that those witnesses who had appeared earlier at the inquest were consistent in their testimony before the jurors.

The next morning, Sheriff Long again arrived at the jail to pick up his prisoner, this time to deliver her to the courthouse. The sight of the lawman walking Bessie to the door brought a rush of onlookers to the courtroom, which was immediately packed. Every seat and every foot of standing room was filled within minutes. Some even climbed on the rear benches to get a better view. "Many ladies," according to the *Calvert Journal*, "occupied seats in the courtroom and were interested witnesses of the proceedings." No case upon the records of the court in recent years had excited more interest in Calvert County.

To no one's surprise, the grand jury had decided that the charges against Bessie Condiff were supported by the evidence. The indictment charging her with the murder of her husband, Littleton T. Condiff, was filed the same day. The *Calvert Journal* described the scene as the indictment was about to be read:

> *The prisoner is a middle aged woman...*
> *possessing a rather strong face...Her*
> *manner was composed and dignified*
> *and her self-control perfect. Her whole*
> *appearance made a favorable impression*

upon the large number of spectators present, including several ladies who happened to be in the courtroom.

Bessie, the report continued, was attired in a mourning costume, wearing a heavy, black veil, which, when thrown back from her face, formed a striking contrast against her complexion, "whitened by her confinement and mental strain." She was described as sitting "calmly," waiting for the arraignment, and when the clerk directed her to stand up and hold up her right hand:

She promptly responded and without displaying the least agitation kept her eyes fixed calmly but intently upon the clerk while she listened to the terrible charge against her.

The Grand Jury's verdict, delivered in the archaic but meticulously precise language of the judicial system, was read by the clerk:

The Grand Jurors of the State of Maryland for the body of Calvert County, do on their oaths present, that Bessie Miller Condiff...on the thirteenth day of September in the year Nineteen hundred, with force and arms...in and upon one Littleton T. Condiff...feloniously, wilfully and of her malice aforethought, did make an assault, and that the said Bessie

Miller Condiff, with a certain pistol then and there loaded with gunpowder and one leaden bullet...feloniously, wilfully and of her malice aforethought, did discharge and shoot off against and upon the said Littleton T. Condiff, thereby striking, penetrating and wounding the said Littleton T. Condiff in and upon the right side of the head...immediately over the right eye ball...and inflicting... one mortal wound, of which...he did languish, and languishing, did live. On the fourteenth day of September...he...of the said mortal wound died.

To the formal question addressed to her at the end of the charge, she was described as calmly answering "Not Guilty" before resuming her seat. During the entire ordeal her countenance did not change, according to the newspaper, nor did her manner indicate the least trepidation. This trial clearly would be nothing like either of Clementine Reckard's.

The next defense move surprised most in the courtroom. Attorney John Gray, after requesting a jury trial, immediately filed a motion for removal of the case on the grounds that his client could not get a fair trial in Calvert County. Bessie is again described as "calmly" and with a steady, firm hand signing her name to the petition. The Court, after a few moments consultation, ordered the proceedings to be transferred to the Criminal Court for Baltimore City for trial.

The Court also directed the sheriff to take the prisoner back to the Prince Frederick jail, to station guards at the windows (according to the newspaper "to prevent persons from interviewing her"), and to take her to the Baltimore City Jail the following day to await her trial. The sheriff left for Baltimore with Bessie the following morning.

A local paper reported that the removal of the case was quite a surprise to many, as well as "a little disappointing to those who wished to hear the proceedings and quite so to the taxpayers who believe the cost to the county will be considerably augmented by the removal." The *Calvert Journal* then made a statement that was surprising itself in light of the sentiments —including suggestions of lynching—expressed in the days immediately after the murder. "The general impression among those present," reported the newspaper, "was that the prisoner would have had a fair trial here and probably stood a better chance of acquittal, which impression appears to be well founded, owing to a sentiment favorable to her."

If there were any sentiment favorable to Bessie Condiff, it was never reported by any of the half-dozen newspapers that covered the case. The *Sun*, in fact, had included in one of its first reports, "The whole island believes the woman guilty and the feeling runs high." Solomon's Island, according to the daily, had already convicted Bessie Condiff.

A CRITICAL DECISION

Facing the Gallows

*In the end, one needs more courage
to live than to kill himself.*

—Albert Camus

No diversion, not even family visits, could lift the pall that darkened Bessie's every moment in the Baltimore jail, even invading her sleep. It was a mantle woven out of the knowledge that there were only two possible outcomes if she were convicted of either of the alternative charges the state's attorney intended to present to the jury. The penalty for murder in the first degree was mandatory: death by hanging. For second-degree murder, a crime found to have been committed without premeditation, the penalty was imprisonment in the Maryland State Penitentiary for up to life. These were the terrors that forced her to turn away from most of the meals put before her, and the sockets of her pale blue eyes to deepen as though morphing into black holes.

No woman had ever been hanged in Maryland. But the most famous hanging of a woman had taken place not far away, in Washington, DC, less than a half century earlier. That was the execution of Mary Surratt in 1865 for her role in the assassination of President Abraham Lincoln. Hangings in Maryland were conducted in the open, a public spectacle, with photographers allowed to capture the moment with their cameras. They weren't conducted in private until well into the 20th century, when they were moved inside the penitentiary. Bessie's stomach churned and her head seemed to spin at any thought of becoming a statistic—or even worse, a photograph—in this bleak history.

Deciding Defense Strategy

Two theories about Capt. Condiff's death had been presented at the inquest conducted by Coroner William Files in September, 1900. The first, the scenario painted by the widow—that he'd been shot by an intruder—had been quickly rejected by the coroner's jury for lack of any evidence. The second theory was that Bessie herself had pulled the trigger. This was the conclusion vigorously advanced by the prosecutor, concurred with by the jury, and according to the newspapers, the one on which "everyone" on Solomon's Island agreed.

There was some talk about a quarrel between the couple in the hours before midnight over several hundred dollars in allegedly stolen money, but the "motive" widely seized upon was the captain's life insurance policy. Underlying this prosecution theory was that clue provided by the couple's next-door neighbor, Mrs. Jane Webster, who ultimately became a key witness. She told the jury that just hours before the murder, Mrs. Condiff had come to her house very worried. Bessie had heard that a number of Solomon's men had dropped out of the Heptasophs, the popular fraternity that had issued Capt. Condiff's life insurance policy in the amount of $2,000, a very large sum indeed in 1900.

If, as Janie Webster testified, Bessie Condiff had told her the day before the shooting that she had a heavy burden on her mind and did not know what she would do, there were many things to which Bessie could have been referring. One dilemma could have been whether or not to continue paying the periodic (almost monthly) assessments for the insurance policy when the money could be used for food. The family was also behind on mortgage payments. She may have been considering a direct inquiry of the fraternity about its financial status. Her husband, after all, had once been the conclave's treasurer; surely someone would reveal whether there were any solvency issues. To jump to the conclusion that the waterman's wife, the mother of his five children, was weighing whether to kill him for the insurance money was about as great a leap as anyone could take. But many did.

The Risks of a Third Defense

When the trial began, Bessie's attorneys put forth a third defense, the possibility that Capt. Condiff might have committed suicide. Up until just three weeks earlier, it was a defense with a huge financial risk for Bessie and her children. The Heptasophs were fighting a court battle over whether the fraternity should have to pay benefits when death was by suicide, which was decried by the order, but at the time not specifically excluded under its life insurance policy. As a high-ranking official of the fraternity had recently put it, "We have the right to require that our members observe the law of God and of man. We should see to it that our membership does not suffer inequitably from losses occurring from the violation of the highest law—that of self-preservation."

In 1900, a lawsuit had been filed against the Baltimore conclave of the Improved Order of Heptasophs demanding payment of benefits under a life insurance policy purchased by the plaintiff's son, who had committed suicide. The Heps lost the suit in Baltimore's Superior Court and appealed. The case was decided by the appellate court on February 8, 1901, just weeks before the start of Bessie's trial.

According to the court's summary of the case, Miles Tull, a young man living in Somerset County, on Maryland's Eastern Shore, was admitted as a member of the Marion Conclave of the Heptasophs on August 3, 1898. He applied for and was granted a benefit certificate for $5,000, for which he paid the sum of $2.50, on August 5. On or about August 4, he declared that he was going to Baltimore to get a job, and that if he did not get one, he would never return home alive. He did not get a job, and on August 18, he killed himself with a pistol shot. The fraternity refused to pay out the benefits under the policy, and the beneficiary, Tull's father, sued. The lower court held that when a life insurance policy contains no provision excluding death by suicide, and it is not shown that the insured obtained the policy with the intention of committing suicide, then the insured's having killed himself while sane was not a defense to an action on the policy. The burden, furthermore, of proving such intent was on the issuer of the policy.

The Heptasophs were much dismayed by the appellate decision and took measures to protect the society in the future by specifically excluding benefits in cases of death by suicide.

Attorneys Thomas and Gray, however, were relieved by the opinion, coming on the eve of trial, when they were fine-tuning their defense. Now they could put two theories before the jury, without concern that one, while saving their client from the gallows, might also leave the widow and her children penniless. Since there was no question about Capt. Condiff's intent when he purchased his policy two years earlier, the Court of Appeals decision cleared the way for them to raise the possibility of suicide without a potentially devastating financial risk to their client.

Shortly afterward, the State's Attorney's office announced that the trial of Elizabeth Tarlton Condiff would begin on February 27, 1901.

11

HER LIFE AT STAKE

SOLOMON'S ISLAND TRAGEDY

*Striking scenes in court as the island woman
is brought to answer for the homicide*

The high temperature for the penultimate day of February, 1901, was just above freezing, but Baltimoreans were grateful at least that no snow was in the forecast. January, typically the city's coldest month, had spread 6.5 inches of the white crystals across the landscape, but February brought less than 3 inches. The citizens dismounting from buggies in front of the new courthouse at nine o'clock that Wednesday morning were dressed for the winter weather, whatever it wrought by the end of the day. But the chill in the air was the least of their concerns. They had come to witness a spectacle such as they'd never seen before in their lives. And to most, the theater in which it would play out was itself a revelation.

Just fifteen years earlier, the city of Baltimore had taken the first steps toward building a "temple of justice," a courthouse second to no other in the world and by far the most beautiful in the whole United States. Now, with its huge, brass doors open for just over a month, the grandiose building humbled its visitors at first sight with its white marble facade, punctuated by eight of the largest monolithic columns in the world, each cut from a single stone and more than 35 feet in height. While the Renaissance Revival architecture was born in a place and time both foreign and far away, the structure itself was an embodiment of Maryland's core, from its Howard County granite foundation to its walls of Baltimore County marble. Inside, a visitor was enveloped in beauty, including sixteen more columns of Italian marble, English oak walls, a barrel-vaulted ceiling, stained glass skylights, and murals depicting Maryland history. Two domed, stained-glass skylights introduced the goddesses of Justice, Mercy, Religion, Truth, Courage, Literature, Logic and Peace. The building clearly was intended to be a monument, not to any man but to the rule of law.

The visitors from Solomon's Island, and many of the spectators from Baltimore as well, most of whom had never seen anything like it in their lives, gawked wide-eyed at every turn. All except one. When the spectacle had ended, no one could recall any moment when Bessie Condiff's eyes wandered away from the players taking the witness stand in front of her, and certainly not to gaze at the grandeur of the setting in which her agony was unfolding.

Criminal Court No. 1 was filled with spectators by 10 a.m. when the clerk called the assemblage to order as Judge Peregrine Lithbury Wickes ascended to the bench. A dignified and respected jurist, Judge Wickes had served on the Supreme Bench of Baltimore City since 1891.

On this winter morning, the mustachioed, silver-haired judge was about to preside over a trial that all of Maryland would be following, including the throng of visitors who had come to the city by steamboat from Solomon's Island. Former friends and neighbors of the defendant and her deceased husband were scattered throughout the packed courtroom, either as witnesses or spectators. They made no effort to hide their awe at the beauty and majesty of the courthouse, some even roaming about the halls during a recess, stopping to stare at oil paintings, and peeking into every open door. One woman carried a baby, at times feeding him from a bottle to quiet his crying during the proceedings. Sitting heavy-hearted among them was Bessie's mother, Mary Tarlton, watching every moment with crippling anxiety. Bessie's elder daughter, Mary, and her husband, who lived in Baltimore, were there, too, along with other relatives. Many Baltimoreans with no connection to the case also clamored for admission to the proceedings but were refused. Among the exceptions, according to a *Baltimore Sun* report, were "a number of well-dressed ladies."

All eyes were on Bessie, many straining for a view over other heads, as she was brought into the courtroom from the lockup. She was dressed in mourning, with a long black veil that concealed most of her head from view, and black kid gloves. She removed the veil as the charges were read, and did not put it down again for the rest of the day. According to a reporter, "prison life," more than five months incarceration to be precise, told on the woman, showing in the "extreme pallor of her face." She was thin, he noted, her chin small and pointed, her cheekbones prominent, her eyes blue and "somewhat sunken." He also added, a bit sympathetically it seems, "she is the mother of five living children."

Other than the infant's occasional fussing, there was barely a sound in the courtroom as the clerk asked, "Are you Bessie Miller Condiff?" Bessie's voice was calm and even as she answered, "I am."

The clerk then read the indictment charging the widow with willfully, deliberately and with premeditation murdering her husband, with malice aforethought. When asked, "How do you plead?" she answered in the same low, calm tone, "Not Guilty." She was expected, at this point, to enter her request for a jury trial, but had to be prompted by her attorneys.

Only then, as she took her seat at the defense table, did there seem to be even the expulsion of breath from the crowd, so riveted were they on every spoken word. Bessie seemed oblivious even to their presence, so focused was she on every next step. From that moment on, the defendant appeared totally absorbed in the proceedings, at times leaning forward as if to see or hear better, but never relaxing her gaze. Her face remained expressionless except at rare intervals when she smiled slightly while talking with her attorneys. "All her senses," wrote the *Sun's* reporter, "were absorbed in the trial." And why not? As succinctly stated in his headline, her life was at stake.

Jury Selection

Choosing a jury was less challenging for this trial than it had been for the much publicized second Reckard trial. Bessie's attorneys were particularly relieved to have no difficulty finding twelve men from among the regular court panel who claimed to have formed no opinion about the Condiff case. Nor did the prosecution have any difficulty finding enough jurors who admitted to having no conscientious scruples against convicting a woman on a charge that would end with her hanging. It took just twenty minutes to seat twelve jurors from the first twenty-three of twenty-five to be screened. The members, whose names, as was the custom, were published in the newspaper, included a conductor, a flour and grain commission merchant, a paperhanger, a grocer, a confectioner, a plumber, and other tradesmen.

The Prosecution's Case

The State of Maryland was represented by Baltimore's Deputy State's Attorney Edgar Allen Poe (a second cousin of the poet), State's Attorney J. Frank Parran, and William Hellen of Calvert County, the latter two having worked the case from the beginning. Mr. Poe made the opening statement for the State, while defense attorneys Gray and Thomas reserved theirs until the State had closed its case.

Mr. Poe seemed at first to be trying to put the jury at ease, saying that although the case was a serious one, their approach to deciding it should be the same as in an ordinary case of, for example, larceny. The State's goal in presenting the testimony of the witnesses would be to prove a willful, deliberate, premeditated killing: a clear case of murder in the first degree. He acknowledged, however, that the State's case was founded almost entirely on circumstantial evidence.

The First Witness

The first person to take the stand in a murder case can be a mere scene setter for later, more potent witnesses, or the biggest shot in the prosecution's arsenal. Dr. William H. Marsh, Solomon's resident physician, was a cannonball. He took the stand at 11 a.m., and launched directly into his lurid narrative.

Dr. Marsh testified that he had been called to attend to Capt. Condiff after the waterman was shot, arriving at his bedside about 12:45 a.m. on September 13:

> *I found he had been shot through the right eyelid. The bullet entered above the eyeball and passed upward and backward to the left side of the skull. There was considerable powder on his face and his right eyebrow and right eyelash were scorched. He was lying on his back when I saw him first, with his head turned slightly to the left. His right eye must have been closed when he was shot. He was unconscious and remained so until he died, about 2:25 p.m. on September 14.*

There wasn't a sound in the courtroom as the prosecutor directed the witness to continue:

> *The pistol could not have been more than six inches from Capt. Condiff's head when fired, and it must have been fired from his right side. It was impossible for anyone standing on the outside of the room to have fired the shot through the window.*

During an autopsy after Capt. Condiff's death, Dr. Marsh said he had found the bullet, which he recognized as of .32 caliber, in the dead man's brain. He further testified that when he'd arrived at the house, he found Mrs. Condiff sitting at the head of the bed, moaning:

> *I asked her if there was a pistol in the house. She replied, "No. Someone must have shot Littleton for his money." She exclaimed, "See if you can find the money." No money was found. Her actions were decidedly quieter than they had been in cases of death in the family before.*

The physician did not identify the other deaths to which he was referring, but observers assumed it was the two children Mrs. Condiff had lost before or during childbirth.

Cross-Examination

The defense pressed Dr. Marsh on a number of issues, including how he could be certain the gun found in the yard a couple of days after the shooting was the one used to kill Capt. Condiff. He replied that the bullet he'd found in the deceased's brain had been scraped, and that he had found the particles of lead in the pistol. Another question was how he could be so sure that the shot was fired from the right side (which was Bessie's side) of the bed. He

answered that for the shot to have been fired instead
from the left side, "it would have been necessary for
the person firing the shot to have fired it with the left
hand and to have reached over Capt. Condiff's body."

On redirect examination, the physician said he
was aware that Mrs. Condiff was the beneficiary
of a $2,000 life insurance policy issued by the
Heptasophs, and that she personally had sometimes
paid the assessments for the policy, taken out about
two years earlier.

The Neighbors' Accounts

The prosecution's second witness was a waterman,
Capt. J. Wesley Lusby, a nearby neighbor who said
he'd been awakened by the noise of the shot and
then heard "a kind of squeal." He continued that
both he and his wife got out of bed and after quickly
dressing, arrived at the Condiff's house within ten
or fifteen minutes to find out what was wrong. Capt.
Condiff, he said, was lying in bed, covered up, and
Mrs. Condiff was beside him, dressed. It was a
bright, moonlit night, he continued, and "I saw no
one leave Capt. Condiff's house except his son going
for a doctor."

The next day, according to Capt. Lusby, "Mrs.
Condiff got some money out of her underskirt and I
counted it for her. It amounted to exactly $100. There
were six $5 notes and seven $10 notes."

His wife was next on the stand. Mrs. Lusby also
testified about the money, saying that Mrs. Condiff

had told her that Capt. Condiff had $255, of which he'd given her $100 to use and had put $155 in a shot bag under his pillow. She corroborated her husband's testimony about Bessie having taken bills from her underskirt for him to count, adding that Bessie had then given the money to her son to keep in case anything happened to her. Mrs. Lusby also testified that a day or two after the shooting Mrs. Condiff had told her she would have to get strength to fight the battle, as she thought suspicion would rest on her. Mrs. Condiff had realized this from a look given her and remarks made by Mrs. Kate Condiff, the wife of Capt. Condiff's younger brother, George. Those remarks called for lynching whoever had killed the waterman—whether man or woman.

Another neighbor, Mrs. Janie Webster, told the same suspicion-raising story she'd told at the inquest and before the grand jury about Bessie coming to her the day before the shooting. She repeated that Bessie had asked about the status of the Heptasophs, the fraternity that had issued her husband's life insurance policy, adding that she had a heavy burden on her mind and didn't know what she would do.

The Gun

Next on the witness stand was Perry Evans Jr., who identified the pistol that was allegedly used to shoot Capt. Condiff. He testified that he had sold the gun for 50 cents to Capt. Condiff's teenaged son, Harrison, at Christmas, 1899.

The gun had been found after the inquest by watermen John Railey and Clarence Greenfield, Capt. Condiff's son-in-law, who corroborated each other's testimony that the rusty pistol had been lying in the grass in the yard of the Condiff house, and that they had led a detective to it. It contained, they said, one empty shell, two unexploded cartridges and two empty chambers.

Winding Up

The final prosecution witnesses included William H. Crockett and Capt. John F. Webster, who testified about the financial affairs of the Condiffs. The latter was owner of Webster's Store, the general store on Back Creek in Solomon's, where island residents could buy almost everything they needed, and credit was generously extended in hard times. He also held the mortgage on the Condiff home. The deceased waterman, according to this testimony, had a large tab at the store, and was also seriously behind on mortgage payments. Sheriff Harrison C. Long testified about his search of the Condiff home after the shooting, and William H. Hellen, one of the prosecuting attorneys, testified about Mrs. Condiff's testimony at the inquest. There was nothing new in any of these accounts.

At this point, the prosecution rested.

12

THE DEFENSE
FIGHTS BACK

A jury consists of twelve persons chosen
to decide who has the better lawyer.

—Robert Frost

With the State having rested its case, attorney John Gray made the opening statement for the defense. Standing before the jury, he laid out possibilities the prosecution had not asked them to consider. The defense would show, he stated emphatically, that the death of Capt. Condiff could have resulted from suicide, or perhaps a shot from a burglar. He would also show through the testimony of witnesses "that the relations between Capt. Condiff and his wife had been the most friendly imaginable in all of their married life" of twenty-four years.

Bessie's mother, 72-year-old Mrs. Mary Tarlton, who had been living with the family on Solomon's Island on the night of the shooting, was the first witness for the defense. She told the court that she had never known Capt. Condiff and her daughter to have had cross words. Bessie, she testified, was subject to epileptic spells, and had been in a very nervous condition.

She related how the couple had been sitting on the back porch at about seven or eight o'clock on the warm Wednesday evening before the shooting. When she went to join them, she overheard part of their conversation. Capt. Lit spoke of some money he intended to invest in oyster planting. His wife said she did not approve of spending it that way. Capt. Lit then remarked that he had always been unlucky and said he believed it would be best if he were dead. His wife, according to her mother, responded, "We can't die when we want to," to which the captain allegedly replied, "Well, we can kill ourselves."

There was some stirring and audible murmuring among the spectators as the elderly grandmother returned to her seat in the courtroom.

The Son Testifies

According to the *Baltimore Sun*, Bessie's eyes were riveted on Harris, the next defense witness, as he "answered boldly" the questions put to him by attorney Gray. From time to time she slightly nodded her head as the 17-year-old testified. He stated that his parents had always been on affectionate terms. As for the pistol, he testified that he had bought it for 50 cents at Christmas, a year ago. "It was no good," he continued, "and after a week or so I took it to pieces and threw it away."

As he had testified at the inquest, he stated that he had been out fishing Wednesday evening and had returned home about 9:30 p.m. He said he went to bed without seeing either his father or his mother:

> *All the doors and windows of the house were open, as was the custom all through summertime. I slept in a room to myself over the kitchen and was aroused by a shot about 12:30 or shortly after midnight. I heard my mother call me and I rushed downstairs. She was coming out of the bedroom. I lit a lamp and went to my father's bedside. He did not speak, but put his left hand on my shoulder. I then went for a doctor.*

In response to a question from defense attorney Gray, Harrison said he did not think it possible for his mother to have thrown the pistol out of the door of the house during the time that elapsed between the moment he had heard the shot and the moment he met his mother coming out of the bedroom.

A Daughter Bears Witness

The defense then called to the stand one of the defendant's married daughters, Virgie, Mrs. Andrew Johnson, attired in mourning like her mother. Calm and dignified, she spoke of Bessie's character, describing her as a good wife and excellent mother. When questioned about Capt. Condiff's health, she said that for the past few years her father had not been of his usual cheerful disposition. Asked by defense attorneys about the gun, Mrs. Johnson said she had never seen her mother with a pistol. She also testified that before her father's death, he had placed his arm affectionately around his wife, who was "nearly prostrated."

The death bed scene was also described by Albert Tarlton, Bessie's brother, who lived on Solomon's Island, and attested to the couple's affection toward each other. Bessie was at the captain's side, he testified, kneeling on the bed, moaning and gazing straight into his face as he lay dying. "I thought when the breath went out of him, that the breath would go out of her." He said he'd picked his sister up and carried her from the room after her husband died.

Mr. Tarlton's testimony also addressed the possibility of the shot having been fired from outside the house. He described two grape arbors, one within 8 feet and the other 10 feet of the house. Either of them, he said, would have been enough to conceal a person in the dark.

This testimony was the last for the day. The court adjourned at 4 p.m. with more than a half dozen witnesses for the defense yet to testify. The jury would spend the night in the courthouse dormitory.

Day Two: Dueling Doctors

The jurors returned to their seats in the jury box the next morning at 10 o'clock. The first handful of witnesses called by the defense testified along the same theme as the last heard the day before, describing the affectionate relations that the Condiffs had always exhibited toward one another.

There was more stirring and whispering in the courtroom when the next witness was called. Jurors and spectators alike seemed keen to hear the testimony of Dr. Charles G. Hill, chief physician of Mount Hope Retreat, a Catholic-run mental institution founded in Baltimore in 1840. Dr. Hill was an "alienist," a psychiatrist who specialized in the legal aspects of psychiatry. Well known and respected as a professor of nervous and mental diseases, he was frequently called as an expert witness on the question of whether a defendant was legally competent to stand trial. He often appeared in homicide cases. It was not clear what his purpose would be in this trial, since there had been no suggestion at any time that the defense might claim that Bessie Condiff was insane or otherwise incompetent to stand trial.

It was no wonder, therefore, that the respected psychiatrist had the attention of every soul in the courtroom as he raised his right hand to take the oath. There wasn't a sound among the spectators as he took his seat on the stand beside the judge's bench.

After establishing in considerable detail the witness's credentials, Attorney Thomas got right to the point. The doctor responded without hesitation or equivocation. It was his opinion that from the nature of Capt. Condiff's wound, the waterman could have committed suicide. Several gasps could be heard from among the surprised spectators in the packed courtroom in the mere seconds before he continued. The captain, Dr. Hill explained, need not have been totally paralyzed by that single, small-caliber gunshot to his brow. In fact, he continued, the waterman could possibly have thrown the pistol away himself after it exploded. Furthermore, he said, the fact that Capt. Condiff's eye was found closed after he was wounded did not necessarily prove that he was asleep when the pistol was fired. Moreover, he added emphatically, "the bullet might have been fired from any direction, according to the position of the dead man's head."

The courtroom audience's surprise at this statement was audible. Some appeared perplexed, if not stunned. Bessie's handsome, young defense attorney at this moment promptly announced to the bench, "We would like to have a practical demonstration of Dr. Hill's theory."

With a nod from Judge Wickes, Attorney Thomas then called Harris Condiff to the well of the court. He directed the skinny teenager to lie down on the floor directly in front of the jury box. Necks stretched and some spectators even rose from their seats to watch. The judge, focused on the spectacle, ignored the inappropriate behavior near the back of the room.

Dr. Hill stepped down from the witness chair and approached Harris as he lay on the floor. He then demonstrated the various directions and angles from which the bullet might have been fired. The doctor changed the position of Harris' head to correspond to each theory.

It was the only time up to this point in the trial that Bessie showed any obvious emotion. Seeing her son demonstrating the very moments and the positions in which her husband may have been lying when he was shot, her self-possession seemed to melt away. She clenched her gloved hands and lowered her eyes, never looking at what must have seemed a grotesque role-play just a few feet away.

Intent on gauging the reactions of the twelve jurymen, the spectators' eyes darted from each move of the witness prone on the floor to the jury box. Low murmurs could be heard throughout the room until silenced by Judge Wickes' stern glare as he banged his gavel. If Doctor Marsh's testimony had seemed like a cannonball the day before, Dr. Hill's was a bombshell.

The Widow Takes the Stand

Elizabeth Miller Tarlton Condiff, wife, mother, widow, and of late, alleged murderess, took the witness stand at 12:30 p.m. All eyes in the packed courtroom were riveted on the slim woman in black mourning dress. Her veil was drawn back over the brim of her hat; her weatherworn hands hidden inside soft, black gloves. Only her pale and angular face bore witness to the trial that for her had begun five months earlier, with one guilty verdict after another and no opportunity to defend herself.

This was that moment, and although she had struggled to prepare, the strength to make her voice heard simply wasn't there. She answered the questions put to her by Mr. Thomas in a trembling voice, so weak that the jury showed some impatience at not being able to understand her. Judge Wickes, demonstrating the judicial temperament that had become his trademark on the bench, suggested that she be seated directly in front of the jury, 3 or 4 feet from the rail. The clerk quickly placed a chair at the designated spot, and she walked slowly to it, emitting a low sigh as she sat down.

Judge Wickes then took another seat to the left, a short distance from her. The lawyers for the prosecution and defense also repositioned themselves appropriately.

She continued her testimony in a low voice, but gradually raised it as she became absorbed in the task at hand. According to the *Baltimore Sun*, her voice only faltered with emotion when she told of her married life of twenty-four years, during which she'd borne seven children, five living and two deceased. The newspaper reported the rest just as she had testified:

The night in question, my husband and I were sitting on the back porch. He spoke of desiring to buy some oysters [for planting in the oyster beds]. I objected, and he answered that it was just like a woman—always objecting. He got angry. Finally I gave my consent, but I told him the reason I was not willing was because he was so unfortunate. He spoke of killing himself. I told him I did not believe he would do anything like that. I gave him the shot bag in which I kept the money and told him to take what he thought he needed, but to leave me enough for house expenses. When he had taken out some money he gave me back the bag and I sewed it to my skirt pocket.

Before I lay down he put the money he had taken between the bed and the mattress. I have never seen the money since. I said my prayers and went to bed between eight and nine o'clock.

Scarcely a breath could be heard in the courtroom as Bessie continued her narrative:

> *The Captain complained of the warm weather. All the doors were open. Sometime during the night I heard a peculiar noise. I knew not what it was, but my first impression was that Judgment Day had come. In springing from the bed the coverlets entangled my feet. I heard a gasping sound. I think I screamed, though I am not sure. I heard my husband gasping for breath. I then screamed for my mother. My son Harrison rushed downstairs, closely followed by my mother. Harrison said something to me about his father. He then lit a lamp, and as soon as its light struck the bed my mother screamed: 'Oh, he is shot!' Then I fell in a kind of stupor.*

At another point in her testimony, Bessie recalled that her mother had helped her put on her wrapper, stockings and shoes before anyone else arrived. Then:

> *The first thing I remember was the words of Dr. Marsh—'Decidedly a case of suicide.'*

Bessie's tone changed slightly as she recounted events after others arrived:

> *Then I thought about the money. Afterward I remember of asking for a detective. I also remember of going to my husband's side and Mr. Hellen [one of the prosecuting attorneys] coming to me saying: 'You have my sympathy.'*

There was a slight suggestion of bitterness in the last statement, that tinged the following as well:

> *Mr. Hellen told me there was a detective who wished to see me alone. I saw him and I found out he was for the State. I told him a full story. He said, 'You may tell that yarn to these greenhorns down here, but you might as well own up to it. You did it yourself.'*

Once again there was a murmur among some of the spectators, presumably since some may have considered the detective's alleged reference to "greenhorns" a slur against them. Bessie then recounted how Detective Spandauer, while accompanying her to the jail in Prince Frederick after her arrest, had told her, "You'd better make a confession, save the State expense and thus induce them to be easier on you." And then, for the third time, insisting, "You might as well confess it, as we have enough evidence." Bessie said that she'd told him she could not tell a lie:

> *I dearly loved my husband. We were always affectionate. He never uttered an unkind word. [Here, according to the Sun, her voice trembled with emotion.] I did not shoot my husband. I would not have hurt him to save my life. I did not want to even mention in my testimony about my husband being melancholy and threatening to kill himself, but my attorney, Mr. Thomas, told me to tell the whole truth, and I did so.*

Bessie also rebutted the testimony of the neighbor who'd been a key witness against her at the inquest, as well as before the grand jury:

> *As for Mrs. Webster's testimony, I never said a word to her about my husband being insured by the Heptasophs, so help me God [raising her right hand as in the act of taking an oath]!*

The second motive argued by the prosecution involved the money that Capt. Condiff had insisted his wife give him from the purse (a shot bag) she held in a pocket sewn into her underskirt. She said he wanted to invest it in oyster beds. In response to her attorney's further questioning about that, the widow claimed that the couple considered it their son's money:

My husband always brought me his earnings, which I kept in the half of a shot bag. We had been saving up money quite a while, and it was looked upon by us as being our child, Harrison's, money. The Captain wanted to buy him a boat, and therefore never considered it his own money.

Finally, when speaking of the Captain's death, she became emotional again:

I was present with him when he died. I was right alongside of him, calling him to speak to me and praying for him.

There was a brief pause at the conclusion of Bessie's testimony to give her a moment to compose herself before Mr. Poe began his cross examination. He focused on one thing: the money. His first question was about the life insurance policy, and she acknowledged that she knew her husband was insured for $2,000 by the Heptasophs fraternity, and that she was his beneficiary. In response to another question, she stated that when she gave her husband the shot bag containing money, she did not know how much he took out, or how much remained, until the next day. She said there had been $255 in the bag, and when her son counted it after the shooting, he said there was only $100 in it.

Mr. Poe asked what became of the other $155, adding, "It must have been stolen?" Mrs. Condiff said she did not know.

The Defense Rests; The State Rebuts

With the defense now having presented its last witness, the State recalled Dr. Marsh to the stand. He denied having any recollection of saying in Mrs. Condiff's presence that Capt. Condiff's death was a "clear case of suicide." He also acknowledged that he was at the time—and still was—a medical examiner for the Heptasophs.

After a brief recess, Judge Wickes announced at 2:55 p.m. that closing arguments would then begin.

THE VERDICT

*Money has been the most serious handicap
that we have ever met. There are times
when poverty is fortunate.*

—Attorney Clarence Darrow

The attorneys for the State of Maryland and the defense attorneys for Elizabeth Miller Tarlton Condiff addressed the jury for more than three hours after the close of testimony on Thursday afternoon. State's Attorney for Calvert County J. Frank Parran led off, with Deputy State's Attorney Edgar Allen Poe and William Hellen following, speaking for thirty minutes each. Young Tazewell Thomas then spoke for one hour and ten minutes for the defense, followed by chief defense counsel John Gray, summing up in half an hour.

The purpose of the closing argument is to remind the jurors of key facts introduced into evidence during the trial, and then to persuade the panel that this evidence supports the conclusion advanced by that side. It is each lawyer's final chance to convince the jury that he or she should win the case.

Leading off for the State, Mr. Parran might just as well have held up a huge dollar sign, for that was the focus of the prosecution's argument: Money! One after the other, the state's attorneys reminded the jurors that Mrs. Condiff admitted having quarreled with her husband the night he was murdered. They had quarreled, the lawyers mentioned again and again, over some large portion of $255 (the equivalent of almost $9,000 today). This, Mr. Parran and his co-counsel argued, was just one of the motives for Mrs. Condiff's grabbing a pistol that was in the house—a heavily mortgaged house, with payments in arrears—and shooting a husband she considered to be making a foolish decision. To invest in oyster beds, as he was proposing to do, when the industry had been faltering for almost a decade, and his income had declined with it, was a decision she admittedly considered ill-conceived and potentially disastrous for her family's well-being.

Then there was that insurance policy. A payout of $2,000 was more than tempting when facing the kind of poverty the family had been dealing with daily for several years. And continuing to pay those assessments to maintain the policy seemed risky if the Heptasophs were a failing fraternity, which a neighbor claimed the defendant was worried about.

It wasn't that Mrs. Condiff held any malice toward her husband. The state's attorneys admitted that they had failed to show that any malice existed between the two. But there was the issue of money, and the issue of poverty, in the face of which difficult choices had to be made, and Captain Condiff, in his wife's admitted opinion, was about to make a poor one.

Based on these facts, Parran, Poe and Hellen argued that the defendant's guilt was beyond question (although they had earlier admitted and repeated in passing that the evidence in the case was entirely circumstantial). The only question for the jury to decide was whether to deliver a verdict of murder in the first degree if they thought the crime was premeditated, or find her guilty of murder in the second degree if they thought she had acted on an impulse.

Through it all, Bessie Condiff sat motionless, her eyes staring straight ahead or down at her gloved hands, clasped tightly on her lap.

The Defense Rises

This was the first big trial of young Tazewell Thomas's legal career, and he had given it all he had. Now, he stood before a jury that had listened attentively for more than ninety minutes to three of Maryland's most influential attorneys argue that the choice before them was simple: either first- or second-degree murder. He began humbly, almost apologetically, looking each juror in turn in the eye, before arguing that, "with all due respect" to his distinguished colleagues, there was simply a complete lack of evidence presented by the State to connect Mrs. Condiff with the death of her husband.

One by one, he recounted the testimony of the numerous witnesses—not just family, but neighbors as well—who had testified that the Condiffs' was an affectionate relationship, and had been for twenty-four years. A disagreement over money that seemed to have been resolved by compromise (Capt. Condiff apparently had not taken all the money in the couple's savings bag) should not suddenly be seen as the impetus for murder against the background of a harmonious married life of almost a quarter century! And neither should the existence of a life insurance policy for which, it was acknowledged, Mrs. Condiff as well as her husband had paid assessments over the past two years. All of this was conjecture on the State's part; hypothesis—fantasy—fiction—but not fact or conclusive evidence.

And what about the possibility of an intruder? Just because no one was seen near Capt. Condiff's house on the night of the tragedy was not proof that no one was there! Thomas mentioned as an example a recent robbery case in Baltimore that had attracted lots of attention because the thieves had robbed a jewelry store in broad daylight, on a crowded street, and it took weeks to discover who they were. Several jurors chuckled at that.

Then there was the unfortunate possibility of suicide, which no less than an eminent medical expert had testified was in fact a possibility that could not and should not be discounted. Zeroing in on Dr. Hill's dramatic testimony, attorney Thomas reminded the jurors there also had been testimony about the captain's lack of good fortune on the oyster beds over the past several years, his "melancholia" of late, and remarks to his wife during the hours before his death, a conversation corroborated by his mother-in-law.

Then Mr. Thomas took the final, bold step. Looking in succession at each juror as he spoke, he slowly and calmly told the panel there was no second-degree murder verdict to be had in this case. The choice before the panel was straight forward: "Bring in a verdict of guilty of murder in the first degree," he declared, pausing for a moment to be sure they absorbed the gravity of his ultimatum, "or NOT GUILTY!"

The Jury Has the Case

For a moment, there wasn't a sound in the room, all eyes fixed on the faces of the jurors, who gave no hint of how they were leaning or even thinking. With closing arguments ended, the jury retired to deliberate at 6:15 p.m. Mrs. Condiff was led slowly from the courtroom, seemingly spent by the ordeal of the past two days. She leaned wearily on the arm of a deputy warden, as she was taken to the lockup, where she sank in exhaustion on a bench. A few friends and relatives remained in the courtroom, on the chance that the jury might not be out long. Her mother, tired almost to the point of collapse by the day's proceedings, had gone to a friend's house to await the jury verdict.

Suddenly, at around 7:30 p.m, the lawyers received word that the jury had reached a verdict.

They hurried back into the courtroom. Bessie was led back by the same deputy warden. This time she clung to his arm as if to a life preserver, before taking her seat beside her two attorneys.

All rose as Judge Wickes returned to the bench and motioned for the jury to be brought back in. The few friends and relatives who had remained sat with hands clasped together as if in prayer. Then the judge called upon the foreman to read the verdict.

One of the twelve jurors rose and declared in a loud, clear voice: "We the members of the jury find the defendant...NOT GUILTY!

The room erupted in applause. Several people hugged their companions. Tears flooded many eyes and ran down cheeks. Judge Wickes immediately banged his gavel, but the emotions were too raw to quell without a humane moment for their release.

Some were so excitedly sharing their relief that they did not immediately see the drama before the bench. The defendant, overwhelmed, had fainted. According to the *Baltimore Sun* reporter on the scene, Bessie "would have fallen to the floor had she not been caught" by the deputy warden, a clergyman, and attorney Tazewell Thomas, who had been standing by her side. Her family rushed to her as she regained consciousness.

One of the jurors later told the *Sun* reporter that two ballots had been cast. The first was at 6:20 p.m., almost immediately after convening in the jury room. That vote was ten for acquittal and two for conviction of murder in the first degree. One hour later, at 7:25 p.m., a second ballot was taken. That vote was unanimous for acquittal. According to the same juror, "There was some sympathy displayed by the jurymen for the accused woman, but it was soon evident to everyone that the State had failed to prove beyond a reasonable doubt that Mrs. Condiff killed her husband."

14

FAREWELL
TO SOLOMON'S

There are many who will make it very
unpleasant for me, and I dread
the return to my home.

—Bessie Condiff

The *Baltimore Sun* reported that after hearing the jury's verdict of acquittal and fainting, Bessie was taken to the city hospital, where she was treated overnight. The next morning, she was taken in a carriage to the South Baltimore home of old friends, the John P. Clintons, who had known her since she was a child growing up nearby. She was described as being much worse than at any time since her arrest, and unable to speak above a whisper. A tenacious reporter finally persuaded her to make a statement for the newspaper. She stated simply, "I am utterly exhausted and the strain has made me as weak as a baby. I cannot even stand alone. The verdict was a great relief after months of uncertainty and apprehension."

Asked about any plans to return home to Solomon's Island, the widow replied:

I was told today that several women who were my neighbors said they would like to have seen me hang. Although many of the residents of Solomon's Island are my friends and do not believe in my guilt, there are many who will make it very unpleasant for me, and I dread the return to my home. I will remain here for several days yet—in fact, until my nerves are in condition for me to undertake the trip.

If Bessie Condiff ever returned to Solomon's, it may have been only to retrieve some personal items from the family home, avoiding any public awareness of her presence. But there is no record of it, and it is unlikely that she did. The mortgage on that home, held by John F. Webster since 1895, and now seriously in arrears, was assigned to attorney William Hellen (one of the prosecuting attorneys), who foreclosed on the debt in the spring, following the trial. The house was put up for auction and sold for $495, far less than the outstanding mortgage balance of $612. Bessie is identified in the U.S. Census in 1910 through 1930 as living in Baltimore, at first with both Albert and Phillip, and then with Albert after Phillip married and moved to Delaware. She died in 1935.

Moving On

By 1910, Harris had married a Baltimore girl, Laura Vogt, and like his mother and brothers, lived in that city, never returning to Solomon's Island. Nor did he ever take up the demanding life of an oysterman, or any life on the water, which had so driven his father.

The first mention of Harris in the dozen years after the trial appeared in the *Sun* in 1912. It was a society page item noting that he and his wife were guests at a gala farewell reception—with live music and a 10 p.m. "feast"—for a member of the Weems (steamboat) family, who was returning to New York after visiting her sister in Baltimore.

Harris' career path had led to the freight sheds of the Baltimore and Ohio (B&O) Railroad at Camden Station, where he was hired in October 1902, after apparently lying about his age. (His employment record card shows his date of birth as Sept. 29, 1880, instead of 1883. The discrepancy made him 22 instead of his actual 19.) The hustle and bustle of the huge terminal provided the kind of excitement and opportunities that Harris enjoyed. The railroad's five-story warehouse stretched out four entire blocks on South Eutaw Street, next to the Camden Station. According to the B&O, it could hold a thousand carloads of freight at any given time. While initially listed in personnel records under the broad category of "Laborer," eleven years later he was described in newspaper reports as the employee in charge of the railroad's shipment of automobiles.

In the fall of 1913, one particular beauty must have caught his attention immediately. It was an expensive, five-passenger phaeton, a touring car reminiscent of the open, four-wheeled, horse drawn carriages of yore. It had been purchased within the past year by a local socialite, Nanine Brent Sloo, the daughter of a Confederate general, who had practiced law in Baltimore after the war. Now married to a well-to-do New Orleans businessman, she had brought the car back to Baltimore from New Orleans to be serviced while she visited her brother, Duncan Brent, an "attorney connected with the B&O." Mrs. Sloo left for home on Monday, Sept. 29, leaving orders for the Lambert Automobile Company, where it had been serviced, to ship the car to New Orleans.

Lambert's was one of a number of dealers in high-priced cars that had popped up along a half-mile strip in mid-town Baltimore. The automobile had become a status symbol, some costing more than seven times the annual salary of one of the city's steel workers. The ads boasted "every motor car luxury," including electric lights, electric self-cranking, speedometer, clock, 12-inch-thick upholstery, and more. When it came to performance, an ad for the new Hudson 6-cylinder phaeton claimed "A Twelve-Year-Old Drives This Car" as indicative of its "ease of control and responsiveness." Another ad in *The Saturday Evening Post* boasted of the "Stunts the New Hudson Six Will Do." Leading off with "You can drive at a mile a minute," the ad copy continued, "There is a sensation of flying...The nearest thing to it is the feeling experienced in a big car while coasting down a long, smooth hill."

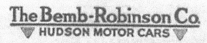

After preparing the car for shipment back to New Orleans (including a thorough polishing inside and out), Lambert's had it driven to the B&O freight yard at Camden Station, where the driver received a bill of lading. But the next twenty-four hours was nothing anyone expected. It did not take Harris long to decide what he would do. Receiving one of these beauties at the freight yard apparently presented a greater temptation than the waterman's son could resist. And he did not. As if on impulse, he put pedal to the metal, pausing only long enough to gather a few friends. Newspaper headlines that Friday told the story:

MYSTERY IN AUTO CRASH

Six Persons Disappear
After Upset on Union Avenue.

POLICE SEEK L. H. CONDIFF

Car Owned by Mrs. Sloo,
of New Orleans, Had Been
Sent to Camden Station for Shipment.

The *Baltimore Sun* report on October 3, 1913 began, "Efforts are being made to arrest L.H. Condiff..." Police claimed that Harris took the car for an outing on Wednesday evening, accompanied by another man, three women (one described as "elderly"), and a boy. Presumably, he thought he could return it without attracting attention. Instead, while driving in the dark around 10:45 p.m., less than five miles from the freight yard, he lost control of the vehicle. It slid down an embankment on Union Avenue and overturned, pinning two of the women under the smashed hood.

Several of the occupants were badly injured, including one woman whom bystanders overheard saying that several of her ribs were broken. Despite these and other obvious injuries, as soon as the passengers were freed from the overturned automobile, the group quickly left the scene without revealing their names. A check with a nearby hospital was fruitless. Harris had been missed from his job at the freight sheds around 6:30 p.m. that day and did not show up for work on the day after. There was no answer at his home.

Baltimore's *Evening Sun* reported that a warrant had been issued for L.H. Condiff—by then known to friends and coworkers as Harry Condiff. The charge was operating an automobile without a license. "Who the occupants were when the car ran down the embankment," the newspaper reported, "is still a mystery."

There were no follow-up articles in any newspapers. The story, with all of its eye-popping elements, disappeared immediately from the pages of the *Sun*. A likely clue as to why is the article's mention of the automobile owner's brother, Duncan Brent, and his connection with the B&O. He was actually a prominent and long-time attorney for the railroad. The theft (or gross misuse) of a large, expensive car entrusted to the B&O, within hours of delivery to its freight yard for transport by the carrier back to New Orleans, was bad enough publicity for the railroad. But the additional admission that the person responsible was the very B&O employee entrusted with such valuable freight was potentially devastating. It is not surprising, therefore, that the warrant issued for L.H. Condiff's arrest did not mention a charge of theft, which would have required the railroad's public assertion of its own employee's wrongdoing and thus the B&O's potential negligence as his employer. Without that, the police could only charge Condiff with driving without a license, which they did.

After firing Harris Condiff the next day, the B&O's first priority was a quick and quiet settlement with Duncan Brent's sister. That is apparently what happened. There is never again mention of Littleton Harrison ("Harris" or "Harry") Condiff in the *Baltimore Sun* or any other local newspapers. Nor is he or his wife listed in the 1920 Baltimore census. When she does reappear in the 1930 census, Laura is listed as a widow. She died, childless, in 1940, at age 52, and was buried near her parents in Baltimore's Loudon Park Cemetery.

As of the night of the crash, Harris Condiff, the 30-year-old waterman's son from Solomon's Island, had vanished.

EPILOGUE

There was never any evidence of an intruder at the Condiff household on that warm, moonlit night in September, 1900 when someone fired a single shot into the head of Capt. Condiff. Besides Bessie and Lit, there were only two other persons known to be in the home. One of them was Mary Tarlton, Bessie's 72-year-old mother. While newspaper accounts described the widowed grandmother as visiting her daughter and son-in-law in Solomon's at the time of the shooting, it appears to have been a very long visit, as she had been listed as a member of the Condiff household on the U.S. Census earlier that year.

Mrs. Tarlton had no perceivable motive for killing or being an accomplice to the killing of her son-in-law, and no attempt was made to link her to the crime. That left Harris, her 17-year-old grandson, who had purchased the weapon, but was never charged with the murder.

The prosecutors—as well as many of the neighbors—had singled out the widow. "Conjecture" was the term used by the newspapers for the theories spun out in the many column inches written about the case as it progressed toward trial. But in the end, a dispassionate jury, far from the murdered waterman's home in southern Maryland, decided *maybe, but maybe not.*

Now, as then, it all remains conjecture. We continue to puzzle over what actually happened on that end-of-summer night on peaceful Solomon's Island.

More than 100 years later, we still ask: Who killed Capt. Condiff?

———————————————

NOTES

CHAPTER 1

OMINOUS FORECAST

page nos.

2 "Warm weather is preventing": *Calvert Gazette*, Sept. 8, 1900, p. 3.

2 "the Nile and Ganges": Ibid.

4 The dredgers persisted. Both Maryland and Virginia now allow commercial dredging with a permit, and under strict regulations for when and where it can be done, and how many bushels of oysters can be collected per day.

5 preventing the poaching: *St. Mary's Beacon*, May 17, 1877, p. 2.

CHAPTER 2

MYSTERIOUS SHOOTING AT SOLOMON'S ISLAND

page nos.

7 "Capt. Littleton T. Condiff": *Baltimore Sun*, Sept. 14, 1900, p. 1.

8 "this is only conjecture": "Died of His Wound," *Baltimore Sun*, Sept. 15, 1900, p. 8.

11 One of these homes: At 14560 Solomons Island Road, the house was wood-framed, described today as a typical "I-house" (a term coined later with reference to its popularity in states beginning with the letter "I") with two interior, gable-end chimneys, and a front-facing gable centered in the roof. Two rooms wide and one room deep, it featured a symmetrical facade, and likely had an el-shaped rear wing for the kitchen. Opposite Solomons Pier, the house has been renovated and added to over the years, including the addition of a front porch. The first floor is currently a gift shop.

12 "finest harbor of the known world": "Letter from Solomon's Island," *Baltimore Sun*, July 27, 1870, p. 4.

13 Notice of Trustee's Sale of Solomon's Island: *Baltimore Sun,* July 10, 1875, p. 3. Isaac Solomon's house, the oldest on the island, at 200 Farren Ave., is today the Chesapeake Biological Laboratory Visitors Center.

16 still in his possession: "Howard County Court - Conviction of a Horse Thief," *Baltimore Sun,* Mar. 26, 1862, p. 4.

19 Members paid periodic assessments: "After the Heptasophs," *Passaic Daily News,* Aug. 24, 1892, p.3. The writer of this letter to the editor claims that a comparison of the costs of a policy issued by the Heps with those of two other prominent fraternal life assurance societies shows the former to be the most expensive, with a $3,000 policy (as an example) costing $22.04 annually (payable in 11 assessments of $2.04 each).

20 "the highest type of civilization": "Heptasophs Held Yearly Service," *Altoona Tribune,* May 4, 1909, p. 2.

20 trustee of the chapter: "Daughters of America," *Calvert Gazette,* June 30, 1900, p. 3.

21 "good order and morality": "Midnight Tragedy," *Calvert Journal,* Sept. 13, 1900, p. 3.

21 the Locust Inn: In 2017, the building was burned down by arsonists, after its Historic District designation prevented the owners from razing it.

CHAPTER 3

THE CORONER'S INQUEST

page nos.

26 Coroner Files swore the jury: "The Wife Arrested," *Baltimore Sun,* Sept. 17, 1900, p. 8. All of the details of the inquest are from the *Sun's* report.

26 up the road from his own: Now known as the Marsh-Beaven House, the home of Dr. Marsh, once also known as The Maples, still stands today at 90 Farren Ave. It included a private medical office where Dr. Marsh treated patients.

CHAPTER 4

A DARK PORTRAIT

page nos.

36 "decidedly queer woman": "Capt. Condiff Shot While Asleep," *New York Sun*, Sept. 18, 1900, p. 1.

37 "at sea as to a motive": "Wife Charged With Murder," *The Washington Post*, Sept. 18, 1900, p. 9.

37 "the reading of dime novels": "Boys Accused of Robbery," *Baltimore Sun*, Sept. 12, 1899, p. 2.

38 "influenced to take the cruise": "Trouble Caused By The Influence of Dime Novels," *Baltimore Sun*, Aug. 28, 1901, p. 6.

38 "Dime Novels Did The Damage": *Baltimore Sun*, Sept. 3, 1891, p. 2. Linkage of youthful crimes with "dime novels" continued into the 20th century. The *Sun* reported in 1910, for example, that police believed a 16-year-old in Roanoke, Virginia who had confessed to shooting a man three times in the head while he slept and robbing him, was influenced by dime novels and Wild West pictures. "Boy Confesses Murder," July 25, p. 10.

39 "sometimes wicked literature": "Dime Novels, An Industry That Is A Mystery To Most Persons," [Fredericksburg, Va.] *Free Lance-Star*, Jan. 12, 1892, p. 1.

39 "better class of readers": *San Marcos Free Press* [Texas], Feb. 16, 1878, p.1.

41 "where the wife lay": "The Wife Arrested," *Baltimore Sun*, Sept. 17, 1900, p. 8.

CHAPTER 5

A HISTORY OF LYNCHING

page nos.

44 "deserving a terrible punishment": *Calvert Gazette*, June 12, 1886, p. 3.

45 When Jones died of pneumonia: "Death of a Respectable Colored Citizen," *Maryland Independent*, Apr. 28, 1899, p. 3.

48 "Some of the Neighbors": "A Double Murder," *Baltimore Sun*, Apr. 25, 1896, p. 1.

50 "to the nearest tree": "State of Maryland," *Baltimore Sun*, May 23, 1896, p. 2.

50 from a nearby bridge: "Cocking Lynched," *Baltimore Sun*, June 29, 1896, p. 2.

51 lynchings in its history: "Lynchings in Maryland," news.baltimoresun.com

CHAPTER 6

UNDER ARREST

page nos.

55 A quarter of a century later: "Maryland County Seats: Today and In History," *Baltimore Sun*, Aug. 18, 1907, p. 15.

55 "The only person in the jail": "The Fire at Prince Frederick, MD," *Baltimore Sun*, Mar. 11, 1882, p. 5.

55 "bathroom in the institution": "Scores Calvert's Jail," *Baltimore Sun*, Aug. 20, 1908, p. 20.

56 "care of the building": "Only Two Rural Jails Rated First Class," *Baltimore Sun*, Aug. 27, 1926, p. 7.

56 "handyman to do the work": "Jails in Four More Counties Draw Blast; Howard's Worst," *The Washington Post*, Feb. 6, 1945, p. 3.

56 to feed prisoners: "County Jails Are Improved," *Baltimore Sun*, Feb. 28, 1955, p. 16.

57 only two meals a day: "County Jail Found Worse," *Baltimore Sun*, Mar. 14, 1950, p. 21.

57 to mend their ways: "Calvert Jail Called Worst," *The News*, Frederick, Md, Mar. 17, 1950, p. 8.

Notes

CHAPTER 7

THE BALTIMORE CITY JAIL

page nos.

60 insured for $2,000: "Mrs. Condiff in Baltimore," *Baltimore Sun*, September 18, 1900, p. 12.

62 "my best to remedy it": "Poverty and Crime," *Baltimore Sun*, August 9, 1898, p. 10.

63 there awaiting trial: "Women in Baltimore Jail," *Baltimore Sun*, August 9, 1898, p. 10.

63 clothes for the prisoners: "An Inside View of the Jail," *Baltimore Sun*, July 14, 1887, p. 4.

CHAPTER 8

HIS DARLING CLEMENTINE: THE RECKARD MURDER

page nos.

68 Azariah Reckard was shot and killed: "Killed in His Bed." *Baltimore Sun*, Jan. 21,1899, p. 10.

69 the eyes of female attendants: "Watched by Women," *Baltimore Sun*, Jan. 23, 1899, p. 10.

69 small quantities of whiskey: "A Sermon on Reckard," *Baltimore Sun*, Jan. 24, 1899, p. 7.

70 a strange scene: "Mrs. Reckard On Trial," *Baltimore Sun*, Apr. 20, 1899, p. 7.

74 "dark red hair": "Mrs. Reckard Smiles," *Baltimore Sun*, Jun. 23, 1899, p. 10.

75 ten years in the penitentiary: "The Highest Penalty," *Baltimore Sun*, Jul. 4, 1899, p. 8. Numerous studies have shown that women are treated less favorably than men at the front end of the justice system but more favorably at conviction and sentencing. But this data has been compiled without consideration of unequal circumstances. Clementine Reckard's light sentence, for example, may have been influenced not only by her insanity defense, acted out in erratic courtroom behavior, but also her

husband's suggested infidelity, and her role as a mother, as well as her beauty, and other gender-based bias.

75 Maryland's state penal institution: "The Rise and Fall of Warden John F. Weyler at the Maryland Penitentiary 1888-1912," by Wallace Shugg, *Maryland Historical Magazine*, Fall 1991, p. 245.

77 released from the Maryland Penitentiary: "Mrs. Reckard To Be Free," *Baltimore Sun*, Nov. 1, 1907, p. 9.

CHAPTER 9

THE GRAND JURY

page nos.

80 "witnesses of the proceedings": "The Condiff Murder Case," *Calvert Journal*, Nov. 17, 1900, p. 3.

80 immediately packed, "The Condiff Murder Case," *Baltimore Sun*, Nov. 16, 1900, p. 8.

82 calmly answering, "Not guilty!": Ibid.

83 "from interviewing her": Ibid.

83 "better chance of acquittal": "Mrs. Condiff Arraigned," *Calvert Journal*, Nov. 17, 1900, p. 3.

CHAPTER 10

A CRITICAL DECISION

page nos.

86 might have committed suicide: "Her Life at Stake," *Baltimore Sun*, Feb. 28, 1901, p. 12.

87 "that of self-preservation": "Order of Heptasophs," *Baltimore Sun*, Aug. 30, 1898, p. 6.

87 According to the Court's summary: Supreme Conclave Improved Order of Heptasophs of Baltimore City v. Miles et al., 92 Md. 613; 48 A. 845, 84 Am.St.Rep. 528 (Feb. 8, 1901).

88 death by suicide: Like most such societies, the Heptasophs would gradually evolve from fraternity to insurance company, losing its fraternal identity completely in a series of mergers with other insurance companies beginning in 1917.

CHAPTER 11
HER LIFE AT STAKE

page nos.

92 Baltimore City since 1891: Upon his mandatory retirement in 1907, Judge Wickes' fellow judges acknowledged his "love of justice and remarkable quickness of perception, and...the accuracy and promptness with which...[he was] able to apply correct principles to the righteous decision of cases." "In Honor of Judge Wickes." *Baltimore News*, Aug. 17, 1907, p. 8.

94 "mother of five living children": "Her Life At Stake," *Baltimore Sun*, Feb. 28, 1901, p. 12. Whatever became of the transcript of the trial is a mystery. It is not in the Maryland State Archives; the only available accounts of the proceedings are from the pages of the *Baltimore Sun*.

95 twelve men from among the regular court panel: Women were not permitted to sit on juries in Maryland until the passage of legislation permitting their participation in 1947.

CHAPTER 12
THE DEFENSE FIGHTS BACK

page nos.

106 Dr. Hill was an "alienist": The title likely derived from the French term "alieniste" for psychiatrist.

110 "The night in question": "Mrs. Condiff is Free," *Baltimore Sun*, Mar. 1, 1901, p. 12. Mrs. Condiff's testimony is quoted from this article, as the trial transcript is missing.

CHAPTER 13

THE VERDICT

121 "NOT GUILTY": "Mrs. Condiff is Free," *Baltimore Sun*, Mar.
1, 1901, p.12. Details of the second day of the trial, from
final arguments through the verdict, are from this article.

122 "killed her husband." Calvert County's bill for the trial, as
rendered by the Clerk of the Criminal Court of Baltimore
City was about $605.75, including $139.52 for the
Court stenographer. *St. Mary's Deacon*, Apr. 4, 1901. (It
was estimated, however, that the entire cost of the case,
including Bessie's board in the Baltimore City Jail, would
likely reach $1,000 (about $35,000 in today's currency.)

CHAPTER 14

FAREWELL TO SOLOMONS

page nos.

123 "I am utterly exhausted": "Mrs. Condiff Faints Again,"
Baltimore Sun, Mar. 2, 1901, p. 7.

124 mortgage balance of $612: In the 21st century, the prime
Solomons Island property would be valued at more than
one million dollars.

125 visiting her sister in Baltimore: "To Say Good-By," *Baltimore
Sun*, Oct. 20, 1912, p. 18.

125 listed in personnel records: Harris Condiff's personnel
record was generously provided by the Hays T. Watkins
Research Library at the B&O Railroad Museum.

126 "an attorney connected with the B&O": "Mystery in Auto
Crash," *Baltimore Sun*, Oct. 3, 1913, p. 14.

130 driving without a license: "Warrant for Driver of Wrecked
Auto," *The Evening Sun*, Oct. 3, 1913, p. 14.

PHOTO CREDITS

Page 4

Oyster Tongers, by Reginald Hotchkiss, photographer. Rock Point, Maryland, 1941. https://www.loc.gov/item/2017745202/.

Page 23

Solomon's Island Public School and confectioner's shop.
Source: Calvert Marine Museum.

Page 26

Dr. William H. Marsh. Source: Calvert Marine Museum.

Page 54

Illustration by Suzanne Shelden based on the newspaper image:
Calvert County Jail, circa 1901. Source: "Maryland County Seats:
Today and In History," *Baltimore Sun*, Aug. 18, 1907, p. 15.

Page 63

Baltimore City Jail. Source: Maryland State Archives.

Page 88

Improved Order of Heptosophs insurance certificate.
Source: Calvert Marine Museum.

Page 91

Clarence M. Mitchell, Jr. Courthouse (Baltimore, Md.).
Source: Maryland State Archives.

Page 92

Judge Peregrine Lithbury Wickes.
Source: Maryland State Archives.

Page 95

Baltimore Criminal Court No. 1. Source: A Monograph of the New
Baltimore Courthouse, 1899 (Frank D. Thomas, publisher);
Baltimore Museum of Legal History, courtesy of Judge William Dunn.

Page 106

Dr. Charles G. Hill, from an oil portrait by Francis P. Wightman, 1905;
donated to the Medical and Chirurgical Faculty of Maryland, 1927.
http://medchiarchives.blogspot.com/p/charles-geraldus-hill.html

Page 127

Bemb-Robinson Co. Hudson Motor Car Ad.

ACKNOWLEDGMENTS

I learned of the Solomon's Island murder while researching the island's history for my book on another Maryland landmark, Cove Point, just six miles north of the crime scene. I wanted to pursue the story when time allowed, but it might not have happened without the enthusiastic support of a friend (and classmate from many years ago), Margaret "Peggy" Kingston. An expert genealogist with a fascination for people and events long forgotten, Peggy dove into this mystery with me, taking us back almost two centuries to Maryland's Eastern Shore.

Another longtime friend, retired Voice of America senior editor Fredrica Depew, provided editorial support throughout our endeavor, which also benefitted from the astute insights of Susan Andross, Teddy Booker, and Peter LaPorte, Director, St. Mary's County Historical Society.

Many thanks for research assistance to the Hon. William Dunn, Baltimore Museum of Legal History; Robert Hurry, Historian, Calvert Marine Museum; Mary Rockefeller, Calvert County Historical Society; Anna Kresmer, Archivist, Hays T. Watkins Research Library; Nate Miller, Reference Archivist, Maryland State Archives; Mary Jo Lazun, Maryland State Law Library; and Karen Boyd and Ronda Libby of Calvert County's Land Records Office.

And what more can be said about the artistry of Suzanne Shelden and editorial brilliance of Sandra Olivetti Martin? I am beholden to you both.

CPSIA information can be obtained
at www.ICGtesting.com
Printed in the USA
JSHW011201050623
42698JS00005BA/24